ROY CLARK

with **Marc Eliot**

My Life

—

In
Spite
of
Myself !

Simon & Schuster
New York   London   Toronto   Sydney   Tokyo   Singapore

SIMON & SCHUSTER
Rockefeller Center
1230 Avenue of the Americas
New York, New York 10020

Designed by Hyun Joo Kim
Manufactured in the United States of America

10   9   8   7   6   5   4   3   2   1

Library of Congress Cataloging-in-Publication Data

Clark, Roy, date.
    My life in spite of myself / Roy Clark : with Marc Eliot.
        p.   cm.
    1. Clark, Roy, date.   2. Country musicians—United States—
Biography.   I. Eliot, Marc.   II. Title
ML420.C537A3   1994
782.42'1642'092—dc20
[B]   93-38364   CIP   MN

ISBN 0-671-86434-3

"Yesterday, When I Was Young" (*Hier Encore*), English lyrics by Herbert
Kretzmer; original French text and music by Charles Aznavour, Copyright ©
1965 (Renewed) and 1966 Editions Musicales, Charles Aznavour, Paris,
France, TRO—Hampshire House Publishing Corp., New York, controls all
publication rights for the U.S.A. and Canada. Used by permission.

"Come Live with Me" by Boudleaux and Felice Bryant, Copyright © 1973 by
House of Bryant Publications.

Acknowledgments

I wish to thank some of the people who played such a big part helping to make this book a reality. For several years, it has been in the back of my mind that one day I'd like to just sit back and remember all the days of my life, both good and not so good. I have done that now, and it has been a very emotional trip. I hope after reading my story, you will come to understand a little more about those many unglamorous moments that have made me what I am today—among other things, so "glamorous!"

First of all, I want to thank Marc Eliot, a terrific writer, and, incidentally, a not-bad guitar player who, because of his impressive knowledge of country music, understood from the very beginning what I was trying to say and was therefore able to put it all into proper focus. I discovered early on I didn't have to stop and explain to him who certain performers were, because he knew them all and the music that they made. We not only worked well together but became very close friends. Perhaps that's why I'm so confident the warmth I feel inside is now on the pages of this book.

I'd like to thank my wife, Barbara, my parents, Hester and

Lillian, and my publicist, Carol Anderson, all of whom spent many long hours going through the thousands of pictures in my personal collection helping to choose the best ones.

In my home office in Tulsa, Oklahoma, I'd like to thank my manager, John Hitt; my secretary-treasurer, Leslie Swindell; John's executive assistant, Mary Thomason; and my administrative assistant, Julia Staires, all of whom helped out in various stages of research.

In Branson, I'd like to thank Taylor Seale, the manager of the Roy Clark Theater, and his staff for their support and Rodney Lay, my bandleader, for his reminiscences.

In Los Angeles, I'd like to thank Sam Lovullo for his generous assistance with the section of the book that recalls the "Hee Haw" years.

In New York, I'd like to thank my editor, Chuck Adams; his assistant, Cheryl Weinstein; and my agent, Mel Berger, who first brought all of us together.

To the rest who played such a big part not only in the writing of this book but in my life, I extend one great big heartfelt thanks, because without them, there'd be no me.

Roy Clark
Branson, Missouri
September 29, 1993

To Lillian and Hester Clark and Barbara Joyce Clark, without whom these pages would be blank.

Contents

Prologue

The opening act has just left the stage. It's intermission now, a few minutes before I'm scheduled to go on. The band is ready, my instruments are tuned and set in place. The audience is in the lobby. Soon the house lights will blink, they'll return to their seats, the curtain will open, and I will take the stage before a theater filled with cheering people who know my name, my face, my music.

A familiar chill snakes up the small of my back to the top of my neck. Someone once said an entertainer has to constantly prove himself all over again, every time he performs; that you're only as good as your next show, and therefore every show is your first.

In the expectant hush before my cue, I bow my head and pray my faith will continue to guide me. I am grateful He has always watched out for me, even when I wasn't always watching out for myself. Perhaps that's why no matter how rough things may have gotten, I never reached a point where I didn't want to go on stage. I've never gotten tired or bored with playing music and entertaining people.

I have a wonderful wife, a great family, terrific friends, and I do what I enjoy before an audience that has stretched around the world. Now, I am ready to make my entrance onto the stage of a theater that has my name on it. Only a few quick steps into the spotlight.

A few steps that took a lifetime's journey to arrive at; a journey that began a long time ago . . .

From a Treble to a Bass

1

I was born April 15, 1933, in Meherrin, Virginia, the oldest of five children. This was the height of the depression, and although my family, like most, did not have very much money, my dad, Hester Clark, always saw to it that we never did without.

Because my dad had to go where there was work, during those years we lived in different parts of the country. He was essentially a sawmill worker, but in reality he did whatever it took to feed his family. He was a proud man, so it wasn't his nature to complain about how things were, or how hard he had to work, even when he was holding down two, sometimes three jobs at the same time.

Before my dad was married, his older brother, my Uncle Kenneth, told him about some work on the railroad that was available in Baltimore. Dad hired on and was immediately sent to Grafton, West Virginia, to work for the B and O railroad in the signal division, putting up and repairing signal lights.

His boss, who eventually became my Grandfather Oliver, was my mother's father. There's a lot of Welsh blood on my mother's side, and her lineage traces back all the way to dukes and princes. It's harder to trace my dad's lineage, because his people were, well, let's say a little loose. He tells stories about my grandfather's daddy, Tom Clark, who used to come and go a lot, but, ahem, didn't leave much of a record. We think he, Tom, came from Ireland.

Anyway, the day my dad first saw my mother on a train, she was with her fiancé. Dad took one look at her and said to himself, "That's the girl *I'm* going to marry." My mother likes to tell how he made a complete fool of himself walking down the aisle clearing his throat, tipping his hat when he did as he tried to get her attention.

Now, because no one could afford to go to a restaurant, the railroad arranged for all the workers in my dad's unit to eat at my Grandpa Oliver's house. Every meal, Grandpa's daughter would come around and put food on the table. When my father looked up that night he saw it was the same girl from the train. After dinner, her fiancé came over and they sat on the porch swing out front. My dad decided to sit across from them. He waited until the fellow went home, and then jumped on the swing himself. Six weeks later my parents were married.

I spent most of my early childhood in Meherrin. When I was six years old I started school. I used to dress in bib overalls with my shirt buttoned proper, all the way to the top. I had only one pair of shoes, and because they were to last me all year, I had to wait to wear them until the weather turned bad. So for a large part of the time I went barefoot, and loved it. I was known to go barefoot in the snow! I was proud of the fact that I had calluses on the bottom of my feet thick enough to let me walk on glass and tacks. All of us kids in Meherrin went barefoot, it was part of our way of life. What I didn't like was when we moved to Washington, D.C., in 1942, when I was eight. I still had only one pair of shoes, and my dad did all the repair work on them. He'd replace the heels and the soles himself. One day they got so bad he couldn't fix them, and because I didn't have another pair, while they were at the cobbler's I went to school barefoot. And the whole school laughed at me. I went home and told my mother I was never going back to school again, at least not until I had my shoes back!

The Second World War was on, and my dad had taken a full-time job at the Washington Navy Yard making lenses for periscopes and telescopes in the optical shop. When his shift ended he would go to work in a grocery store for extra income. That was a break for the family because the owner allowed him to buy slightly discolored meats from the display case at a big discount.

And, in the evenings, he would go on to the one job he really enjoyed. He'd take his guitar and play at Virginia square dances. My father played traditional country mountain string music. He was, and still is, a terrific musician, a master on tenor banjo, guitar, and mandolin. In my opinion, he could have played with the best of them if he had pursued music as a full-time career, instead of letting it just be something he did for fun and to supplement his income.

I have to say, looking back, that in spite of the fact we didn't have a lot of money or material things, growing up in a house filled with music provided me with the happiest of childhoods. When the family would go back to Virginia to visit, my dad's brothers would always be coming over to my grandmother's house, tuning up, singing, and rehearsing before going out to play a job. Soon enough, I started picking up my father's four-string tenor banjo and a mandolin one of my uncles had brought back with him from overseas after the Second World War, and tried to pick out melodies. Even back then it wasn't difficult for me to learn how to play any instrument. For some reason it just came as natural to me as a-walkin'.

I had a cousin, Waymon, my father's sister's boy, who also had a knack for music. We were the same age, just a month apart, more like brothers really than cousins. Sometimes we played a game to see who could pick a song all the way through on the mandolin. The first song I ever remember being able to play was "In the Garden," because it had only three chords. I was seven or eight at the time, and I don't know how much attention I'd have paid to playing at that age if it hadn't been for Waymon. As it was, after a while I'd always put down the mandolin to go out and play ball with the other boys in the neighborhood.

Everybody in the family, it seemed, played an instrument. My mother played the piano, although I hardly ever heard her because we didn't own one. She used to collect lyrics in little spiral notebooks filled with great, classic songs. My sister Jean and my brother Dick both played mandolin and guitar and they were pretty good. I guess the only two who didn't play anything were the babies, Dwight and Susan, neither of whom ever showed any interest in playing music.

One time someone came around from a school and tried to sell my mother a program to teach Jean how to play the accordion. My sister kids me to this day that if it wasn't for me she might have become the "star" in the family. She used to sit there for hours looking at this lesson book trying to figure out how to play the thing. I was intrigued by its sound, picked it up one day and before she got home from school I could play "The Tennessee Waltz." When she heard that, she kind of gave up.

I can understand how she felt. Six hours of practice a day has never bothered me, but six hours a day of practicing "this" would, especially as I always seemed to want to go off and do "that." However, you can't do "that" when you're being taught you have to do "this." I've been able to pick up on so many instruments, guitar, accordion, trumpet, piano, drums, because it comes naturally to me. I can usually play any instrument if I'm shown how, without having to learn the rudimentary steps. Maybe that's what they mean when they say someone is just born with the music already in them.

Another early influence on me was the radio. Listening to country music coming through the static has always seemed a little bit of a mystical experience. I remember as a boy thinking, well, hey, my dad and my uncles aren't the only ones who know how to make that kind of music. There had to be other people who could do it, and that intrigued me. I began to wonder who they were. Did I have more uncles out there?

As it happened, my dad played in one of the first country music string bands ever broadcast over the radio, live over WRVA, an early country radio station, out of Richmond, Virginia. WRVA had put the Tobacco Tags, another local group, on the air live, and they proved so successful, the station sought out other groups. It was all real informal, done without agents or contracts, or for any real pay. I believe this was my dad's one real stab at a career in music.

When I was ten years old, he started taking me to the

free concerts the National Symphony Orchestra played Sunday afternoons in Washington. I remember being bewildered by all that classical stuff. I was used to a mandolin and a fiddler sitting on a porch, not four acres of violinists. When I told my dad I didn't think I was going to like this, he told me not to ever put any type of music down before listening to it carefully. "Don't turn your ears off before your heart hears it. Listen to it." It's something I've never forgotten. Throughout my career I've allowed myself to be influenced by all types of music and all types of entertainers. Thanks to him, to this day I can listen to any music without prejudging it, and will find something of value in almost everything I hear.

I guess every child thinks his parents are the greatest, and I'm no exception. Mine were all and everything I ever needed. I had plenty of love, and a lot of freedom. I had discipline, too, a lot of whippings, and I'm sure I deserved every one of them.

My mother would always say to me, "Wait until your father comes home; I'm going to tell him what you did." I'd go up and sit in my bedroom and wait for him. I'd hear him come in and climb the steps before entering my room and sitting down on the side of the bed to talk to me. First he would tell me why he was going to do it, and then he'd whip me. He was never brutal about it, or angry when he did it. That part always seemed the easiest for me to take. What was hard was the talk that led up to it, because it would make me feel about that big.

Not that I was such a bad little guy. I'd just get in trouble for typical boy things. For instance, I didn't know what a clock was. My mother would tell me to be back at a certain time, and I might be back an hour later. I didn't do bad things, I did stupid things and I was always caught. I threw a bottle one time up in the air, just to hear the noise it would make when it came down. I didn't think about the glass, and it nicked a little girl's leg enough to draw blood. Pure kid stuff.

Everything changed for me when I was thirteen years old and my interest in music began to deepen. I remember the exact moment it happened. We were still living in Washington, and I discovered that a neighbor of ours had a Harmony arch-top guitar. It was a very popular instrument in those days, you could buy one in any music store for seventeen dollars. One day my neighbor heard me picking on my father's banjo and let me hold his guitar. What can I say? It was like the moment in your life when you go from being a boy in short pants to a young man in long ones. It was the first time I'd held an instrument with six strings, from a treble to a bass. I ran a pick down them, and the full spectrum of sound yielded a softness I'd never really heard before. The mandolin was thin and tinny, the tenor banjo *rah-rah,* but the sound of this guitar, well, that was something else. That was the moment I said to myself, hey, there's something here, I have to learn how to play this!

All I wanted now was a guitar. That fall, I got hold of a Sears catalogue and circled the one I really liked. When Christmas morning finally came, I got up early and ran downstairs. Sure enough there under the tree it was, along with a copy of *Smith's Three Hundred Chords for Guitar,* a book of basic chords, orchestra chords, and movable chords. Well, I quickly looked at everything else under the tree that was there for me, said that's great, that's great, that's great, then grabbed the guitar and the book, went back up the steps, into my room, closed the door and started playing.

And I stayed there from sunup to sundown. I played so long the tips of my fingers swelled, and I had to dip them in a glass of ice-water to relieve the pain. I was just starting, so I didn't have any calluses yet. I couldn't wait for my fingers to get tough enough so I could play more. In the meantime, I used the side of my thumb. I was so consumed by playing the guitar, I'd wake up in the middle of the night and start practicing.

I was so lucky, I had a live-in teacher. If I hit a problem, I didn't have to wait a week for a lesson from some music teacher. When my dad came home from work I'd just ask, "How does this go, I see it in the book but I don't understand ..." He'd show me and that was all I needed. I'd have it and go on to something else. Believe it or not, two weeks after Christmas I was good enough to play my first gig at a local dance with my dad.

I didn't, however, play in the school band. I attended Chamberlain Vocational High School on Potomac Avenue in Washington, D.C. I went there because of its commercial art and drafting department, which I was also very interested in at the time. Ever since I first picked up a pencil I was always drawing pictures and doing portraits. The art classes were okay, but I couldn't understand why the school's music teachers looked down on the guitar. At school assemblies, the school orchestra would play things like "Holiday for Strings" with no guitar in the orchestra!

I'll never forget, as far back as mandatory music class at Kramer Junior High School, one day the teacher was defining instruments as either woodwinds, brass, or strings. I can still see her standing there, saying that string instruments were violins, violas, and bass. And I can still feel the sting when one of the kids asked about the guitar and she said, no, the guitar is not a "pure" string instrument, the guitar is a fretted instrument. I felt shot down. For some reason the guitar wasn't "pure." I guess the school considered it a bastard. I never did well in music classes after that. To me, it seemed like it was always a matter of "you will learn this; you will enjoy this," and I remember saying to myself, no I won't, no I can't.

Anyway, even if the teachers didn't, the kids seemed to like the guitar and the way I played it. Because of that I got invited to a lot of parties. It was always, "Hey, Roy, we're having a party this Saturday night, why don't you come." That part was great, until the tag line that inevitably followed, "And don't forget to bring your guitar." To the rest of the kids they'd just say, "Come." I was happy to be invited, but sometimes felt I wouldn't have been if I didn't bring along my guitar.

I did my first TV show with my dad at the age of fourteen in 1947. The DuMont network's local Washington, D.C., station, WTTG, had a show called "The Hayloft Conservatory of Musical Interpretations." Television was in its infancy, and if you could balance an egg on a spoon you could get on a show. I played the guitar and sang a little, so they booked me. I was always billed as "Roy Clark and Dad." It was a little embarrassing to be billed over my dad. I always thought it should be Hester Clark and son. I guess the stations thought it was more of a novelty the other way around. Anyway, the first song I ever performed on TV was "One Has My Heart, the Other Has My Name." I chose it because it was popular, even though I had no idea what I was singing about. I've only experienced real stage fright a couple of times in my career, but the worst I ever had it was when I sang that song. There I was, just fourteen years old, up there in front of the TV cameras. I'll never forget the feeling of having ten thousand butterflies in my stomach, all floating and flying in different directions.

My dad, meanwhile, was still playing square dances, and I guess I had gotten good enough for him to want to start taking me along. These weren't actual "performances" or anything. The only "show" was the dance itself. Everybody in the band just sat and played. We had a microphone, one little PA set, and two speakers with the power unit in between. We either sat on stage or, if there was no stage, in a corner of the room. One mike was plugged into the power unit so the fiddle could play lead with the guitar up close to him, and a second microphone went to the caller. We could set up and tear down our whole operation in thirty seconds.

I usually sat behind the fiddle player and my dad, watching how he played, listening to the tune, and trying to play along. I was far enough back so if I made a mistake it wouldn't affect anything. The fewer mistakes I made, the closer I got to the front, until eventually I found myself sitting right up at the mike.

A fellow by the name of Ralph Case coordinated all the area dances, which included the hiring of the bands. In those years there were often as many as thirty-five square dances a night in Washington. All the friendship houses had them, as did the YMCAs and the military clubs. One night Ralph was at a dance we were playing, and afterwards he went to my dad and said, "Hester, tomorrow night I got this other dance booked, and I tell you what, I'd like Roy to play it." My dad said all right, and the next night Ralph picked me up, took me over there and, when it was over, brought me back.

I was soon playing square dances on my own every Saturday

night, and found I could make four or five dollars for two hours' work. Now I could buy my own shoes, my own school clothes. It wasn't long before I was playing Friday nights as well.

Sometimes Ralph would call me early on Saturday mornings and say there's a radio show goin' on, and could I get over there right away? This one morning Ralph called and told me if I went over to see the station manager of WBUZ, he'd put me right on the air. WBUZ was a brand-new FM station owned by the Washington-Baltimore-Annapolis Bus Company in Maryland. They had acquired their radio license so they could pipe music into their buses.

Now, I didn't know anything about talking on the radio, but they still put me and some other musicians on the air that morning, and every Saturday morning after for many weeks. One of them was a friend of mine and a really good guitar player by the name of Carl Lukat. We had first met the previous summer, through a mutual friend, Smokey Rice. How it happened was, I was working little no-name neighborhood bars, dives, really, around Washington, often with a fellow named David (I don't recall his last name) who played the accordion and another guy who sang. One night David asked if I was interested in spending the summer down in North Beach, on Chesapeake Bay, about forty miles out of Washington, where he hoped to land a warm-weather gig, and earn a little money along with room and board. I told him I'd love to—if I could get my parents' permission. I was still only fifteen years old. It took a little bit of convincing, but finally they let me take the job. Although he didn't want to see me leave home for the first time, it was a little easier to convince my dad than it was my mother. I was the oldest chick about to leave the roost for the first time. I believe my dad spoke to her when I wasn't around, and probably told her that I handled myself pretty well in public and he didn't think I would go astray. I remember when I was getting ready to go, it was as if I were leaving to go off to war. There were a lot of tears and hugs from my mother, and I promised her I would be good.

As things turned out, David and the singer didn't find any work. Smokey Rice, who was a permanent resident of North Beach, had been offered the job that David had been promised, at this small club named Rose's, one of the two main clubs in North Beach back in the days when slot machines were still legal in Maryland. Uncle Billy's, the other club, was the hangout for motorcycle riders. It had the best bands, while Rose's was more of a family place.

Smokey already had a lead guitar player, Carl Lukat, and didn't need an accordion or another singer, but said he could use me because I played the mandolin and could sing harmony. David and his singer left, and I stayed, for forty-five dollars a week and a book of tickets good for one meal a day of certain foods designated okay for the employees to eat. In other words, no steaks. My room was on top of a wooden bath house where men went in, hung their clothes in lockers and sprayed themselves with hose water. What the owner had done was to partition off a series of rooms, stalls really, where the walls didn't go all the way up to the ceiling. If the guy in the next room was thinking too loud, you could hear him.

David and the others wound up returning to Washington, but I stayed in North Beach, playing at Rose's. Carl and I became friends. He was older than I was and really took me under his wing. I learned a lot about playing lead from him, and when the season was over, we came back to Washington together. When I started doing radio, it just seemed natural that he would be part of it. Carl was great moral support, always urging me to try new things, telling me I could do anything I put my mind to.

We didn't know that many songs, mostly Hank Williams, Hank Snow, a little Lefty Frizzell, and some Red Foley tunes. We'd often run out and have to play the same one over a second time. "Hey," I'd say, "that was a good tune we played about thirty minutes ago, let's do it again!" We'd play live as long as we could, then the station put on records. We had this one little amplifier that Carl plugged in. The only AC outlet was up by the door. Carl would plug in, sit there with his guitar and play. More than once we'd be in the middle of a tune, somebody would walk in and accidentally unplug him, and we'd be off the air until he could get his juice back on. Very high tech!

Ralph began booking us to play televised square dances. All I did at first was play. Then someone said, "Hey, we need a song here," and Ralph said, "Let the kid do it," meaning me. Pretty soon I was wearing a big cowboy hat and a black and gray cowboy shirt, fourteen dollar Acme cowboy boots with a square toe on them, and singing not just for the dancers, but the camera, too.

I loved all of it, I couldn't get enough, and pretty soon I asked my dad if I could play more nights. He said no at first, insisting I had to limit my music to Fridays and Saturdays, to make sure my school work didn't suffer. Then one day Ralph called in the middle of the week and said he really needed me for some last-minute gig. My dad gave in and let me do it.

It wasn't long before I added Thursdays to my weekly schedule. Soon Wednesdays followed, which meant that Thursday mornings I wouldn't be able to get up to go to school, and

Fridays, forget it. I then added Tuesdays, and finally Mondays and Sundays. I was making it to school maybe one day a week, if I was lucky. Or, as I saw it back then, unlucky. Those few days I did get there, I usually fell asleep with my head on my desk.

Sure enough, the counselors wanted to know why I was so tired I couldn't stay awake in class. Was everything all right at home? I told them about my music, and how it was often one or two o'clock in the morning before I got to bed. They insisted my school work had to come first, but I just didn't see it that way. I couldn't understand how anything could be more important than playing music.

So I started playing every night. A lot of times I rode to dances with Ralph Case in his 1942 two-door Pontiac. One night he piled seventeen teenagers into the car to go to a dance. I guess being that close, it wasn't hard to find a girlfriend, and I did. Aurelia Baker was her name, she was beautiful and, boy, did I have a crush on her! She sat on my lap during one ride and that was how our courtship began. I went with her for about a year and a half. I'd pick her up at her house and we'd go to the movies. Such great, innocent kid stuff.

A year later I got my first motorcycle, a 1941 Indian Chief. I used to park out in front of the school and wait for girls to come by to ask if I could take them for a ride. Unfortunately for me, none of them did, and now that I look back, it had to be the grossest bike that ever existed, laid over so many times, skinned and beat up, the frame bent so bad it looked like an X going down the road. But, hey, I thought I was king of the hill.

When I wasn't trying to pick up girls, I hung around with guys older than I was. Most of them played music, and some of them were pretty good musicians. They played a lot better than I did, and I looked up to them for that. A lot of them played in clubs, and soon enough, so did I.

Every time I went back to school I was more distressed, until one day, after having missed an entire week, I was walking on my way to school, already late, when I just stopped, turned around, and never went back. I was fifteen and only had half a semester left before I graduated, but I didn't care. The only reason I had stayed with it as long as I had was to please my parents. Now, though, I'd gotten my first taste of the outside world, where I was accepted for what I could do, where nobody cared if I had a diploma, or asked me hard questions I couldn't answer. Music had been the key to a door, and it happened to be the right one for me. As far as I was concerned, I was ready to take on the whole world!

Like any kid, I had dreams of growing up to be a star. Although I didn't know what that really meant, I knew one when I saw one. Hank Williams was a star. I knew, because I not only saw him, but in 1949, when I was still in school, I was fortunate enough to get permission to take a two-week leave so I could work on the same show with him.

That came about because of Connie B. Gay, a promoter who produced a two-week show starring Hank Williams at the Hippodrome Theater in Baltimore. He already had all the stars on the show set, including Cowboy Copus, the Duke of Padukah, Lazy Jim Day, Annie Lou and Danny, and Hank Williams was the headliner. They needed a square-dance group to kick the whole thing off. That was mine. I got in that band, not because of Connie or anybody, but directly through Ralph Case, simply because in that area, if you wanted a square-dance band, he was the man you called.

Ralph Case was one of my earliest and biggest supporters,

so when Grandpa Jones, whose real name is Louis Marshall Jones, set up a four-day tour, Ralph told him, "This kid is really good, you ought to use him." Again, with my parents' permission, I signed on.

The tour was set to travel through Baltimore to just south of Rochester, New York, and needed a guitar player who could sing. I'm sure Grandpa Jones had no idea who I was. Evidently, he was sold on me by Connie B. Gay and Ralph Case. Grandpa Jones was a really big star then, so imagine the thrill I had when the tour was about to begin and he actually came by to pick me up at my home in Washington. Of course, I never in my wildest dreams figured that one day, years later, we would be working together on "Hee Haw."

What set Grandpa Jones apart was his distinct voice. He was only nineteen years old when he had started his career on the radio. Soon the producers began to get letters asking to let the "old man" sing a song. His voice made him sound like he was eighty-five. That's how he came to do his "old man" act.

Back then, in country music, there were terms for every kind of act. If a promoter was putting a show together, he'd want an emcee, a boy singer, a band, and to round things out an "old man" act. A lot of guys would get an old gray wig, black their teeth out, walk out in a shuffle, and in between band set-ups tell "old man" jokes. Grandpa Jones was our tour's "old man."

Because of the success of that tour, Connie B. Gay took me along on a tour with Hank Williams. We played the Hippodrome Theater in Baltimore, one of those beautiful, old, ornate theaters with boxes and velvet curtains in the days when they still alternated a movie and stage show three times a day.

We would open the show, then I'd run right around, sit on the side and watch the rest of it from beginning to end, waiting impatiently until Hank Williams came out. To this day I've never heard anybody able to describe exactly what star quality is, but I can tell you, when he was on stage, Hank Williams had it. All he had to do was come out and stand in front of a microphone and sing, and this "thing" would emanate from him. Offstage, I quickly learned, he was something else.

One day his fiddle player, Jerry Rivers, and I were in one of the dressing rooms, a long, narrow room with lights around the mirrors. Jerry was waiting for Hank to go on, and we started jamming, me on the guitar, Jerry on the fiddle, when Hank came by. Out of the corner of my eye I saw him and said to myself, "Oh my God, there he is." He sat down in a wicker chair, said nothing, and watched us. When we got through playing one tune, Jerry started another, and Hank got up and said, "Well, y'all don't care if ol' Hank's in here or not, so's I might as well leave." With that, he got up and left. I wanted to shout, oh no, stay, please, but I was too scared. When he was gone, Jerry just turned to me and said, "Don't worry, kid. That's just the way he is. If we'd talked to him, he wouldn't have talked back."

Whatever I know now, I learned from watching others. I would see something and try to incorporate it into something I did, not copy, but use it as the basis for making it my own. Or if I heard someone say something, I'd try to turn it around and use it as part of my own. Hank Williams certainly had his share of demons, but what I learned by being privileged to see him on stage so early in my career remains one of the great lessons of my professional life. I can still see him with my mind's eye as vividly as if it were a film playing in my brain, and remember thinking to myself, If only I could acquire even a little of that magnetism he had.

Not long after, I played my first real club date, with Carl Lukat. When the Grandpa Jones gig ended, I returned to Washington. Because I was still only sixteen, I had to get working papers to play in the clubs around Washington, D.C. The local laws stipulated that because of my age, I could not be there before a certain hour, could not stay in the place during intermission, I had to go outside, couldn't linger after and, of course, couldn't have anything to drink.

Our first gig was at the Camden Taverns in northeast Washington. It was a great breaking-in experience for me. The Camden Taverns was one of those fight-your-way-in, play-a-little-music, fight-your-way-out type places. There must have been three hundred bars like the Camden Taverns in Washington at the time, with three hundred little bands to play them, packing them in every night of the week. I say bands, but in reality most were nothing more than a single act, usually just a guy who'd sing and pass the kitty. Sometimes two or three musicians played together and called themselves a band. Anything more than that, you were talkin' orchestra!

Carl played lead guitar, I played rhythm. We did mostly Hank Snow and Hank Williams songs, and took requests from the audience. They'd say, hey, play so-and-so, or they'd come up to the stage and put a quarter in the little kitty. The kitty in those days sometimes got pretty creative. A lot of guys used a waterbucket, with a cardboard cutout of a cat's head attached to the front. Across the can they'd paint "Feed the kitty." Some of them were quite elaborate. Guys would wire them so they'd light up, or had blinking eyes, or were bedpans or slop-jars. Most of the time the band made more from the kitty than they were paid from the guy who ran the place. In our act, we'd say things like, "If you have any requests you'd like to hear, just write it on the back of an old ten dollar bill, and if we don't know it, we'll send you five dollars change."

So there I was, out in the grown-up world at last, a real man! Or so I thought, until I'd go home every night and have to be a kid again. I didn't get it. I felt like, hey, if I'm old enough to play in a club I must be old enough to go to bed whenever I want to, and get up any time I feel like. I didn't realize it then, but I already had one foot out the family door, with the other about to follow.

The other great interest in my life at this time was sports. I was thirty-five years old before I could admit to myself I wasn't going to be heavyweight champion of the world. Up until then, I really believed if I got into serious training and had the right leadership, I could do it. I've always had that kind of confidence in my physical abilities.

As with my music, I owe my interest in sports to my dad. He was a big baseball, boxing, and football fan. When I was a kid he would take me out every night after work and hit ground balls to me. That's how I learned to field—two hours every day, running, catching, throwing, batting. The field we played on was real uneven, and the ball used to take crazy bounces. It got so bad that I was afraid when I played on a professional field I wouldn't know how to field a straight ground ball.

Before I quit high school I played first-string on the Chamberlain team, and local sandlot baseball afternoons and weekends. I was very athletic, with great natural stamina. I even had a chance to try out for the old St. Louis Browns, who later became the Baltimore Orioles.

It's not as if they came looking for me. In fact, they'd sent a scout to check out a pitcher who happened to be a neighbor of mine. "Boots" Pinella was the hero of the neighborhood. He had played with some of the top sandlot teams, and the Browns heard about him and sent a scout to take a look.

Meanwhile, I was becoming a pretty good ballplayer myself. Batting was my biggest asset. I was a strong switch-hitter and could knock the cover off the ball. I can still remember the feeling of hitting one just right—no sting, no rattle, nothing, just a smooth explosion of power. Well, one time this scout came to a sandlot game that I was playing in, down by "the flats," right off the Anacostia River. That day I happened to hit three home runs and a triple.

What should have been a triumph turned into one of my most embarrassing days. I hit the ball and ran to third as the outfielder threw the ball in. I was standing on the bag, winded, but feeling great about knocking in two runs. Then I stepped off the bag to take a lead, thinking the pitcher had the ball, and the third baseman tagged me out. In that moment I went from a king to a dunce. I was so embarrassed to walk back to the bench, I almost turned around and went home.

I guess the scout was sufficiently impressed with my hitting, because he wrote his name on a piece of paper for me with a phone number where he could be reached. He said I should give it to my folks, as he couldn't talk business with me. He did say if I could get to Florida for spring training, the Browns would take a look at me. But, he stressed, I'd have to get down there on my own. If I made the team, they'd reimburse my expenses. Well, I wanted to go real bad, but there was just no way. Florida? That was the other side of the world as far as I was concerned. So that was the end of that.

My dad always came to see my games, whatever sport I was

playing. Besides baseball, I was also on the high school foot-ball team. He really had to make an effort to get home from work on time, because we usually started the game at four or five in the afternoon. I remember one time, in my first year playing for Chamberlain, we had a big football game sched-uled against Eastern High. Well, my dad got off work early, and arrived just as our team was warming up on the field. He had his movie camera with him and wanted to take some pictures, but he couldn't find me. Then, during a lull, he heard the sound of a guitar coming from under the stands. There I was, in full uniform, playing my guitar singing to all the cheerlead-ers! As my dad put it, it was an omen of things to come.

I had also gotten into boxing, although that had come about by accident while I was still in junior high school. A friend of mine had brought me into the Police Boys Club, and I started boxing in tournaments around Washington. With boxing, like my music, I never had any formal training. I conditioned my-self naturally, just by running everywhere I went. After one fight a guy came back to a couple of us and said, "Hey, you want to box a guy for four rounds and make ten dollars?" I said sure, and so for a very brief time I was a professional boxer. We'd fight in bowling alleys, where they'd set up a little ring. I had sixteen bouts that I got paid for, and won fifteen of them.

I was a light heavyweight, 175 pounds, and thought I was serious about it until that sixteenth fight, when I ran into a guy who was *really* serious about it. I believe his name was "Bones" McKinney. He was about six-three, and had arms much longer than mine, which was why I could never get to him. I wasn't a finesse boxer, but I was strong, and that's how I would win. This guy, though, knew what he was doing. He cut my eyes and my face, and that was enough for me. Of course my parents had no idea what I was doing. When I came home all beaten up and they asked what happened, I told them someone had hit me in the eye with a rock.

It wasn't long after my boxing and baseball "careers" ended that I finally did move out of the family house. I figured it was time I was completely free. So what did I do? What I thought every grown-up did. I got married.

I first met Ruby, the woman who was to become my first wife, while I was playing at the Camden Taverns. She used to come with her older sister, Agnes, and a girl she worked with. Ruby was five years older than me, and worked as a waitress in the Hot Shoppes, a sit-down coffee-shop restaurant chain around D.C. and northern Virginia. She was married and had an infant baby girl. Her husband was in prison, supposedly for armed robbery. He really wasn't a professional thief, just a fellow without money caught robbing a store in order to buy milk for the baby.

They weren't divorced when we met, but were separated because he was in prison. I was playing the club, and Ruby started coming by practically every night. Pretty soon we started dating. Our relationship developed gradually. It wasn't a case of me saying, "I think I'm in love with you," "I think I want to marry you," or anything like that. It was more, if I went somewhere, Ruby would just automatically come along. Soon my friends started saying, well, you two have been going together now for quite a while, when are you going to get married? We started talking about it, she filed for a divorce, we set a date, and the next thing I knew I found myself walking down the aisle in church at the ripe old age of seventeen.

My mother and dad, all my brothers and sisters, her family, and all our friends were there, laughing, smiling, having a good time, while I kept saying to myself, what am I doing? Looking back, I think what happened was because I moved away from home at such a young age, I really wasn't ready to be alone. A lot of my older musician friends were alone, but they seemed to like it. I needed someone. I'd come from under the very protective wing of my mother and missed that, which was maybe why I had started going with an older woman in the first place.

So I found myself in the church, getting married, not really wanting to, but afraid of being alone, and also not wanting to disappoint all these people.

No sooner did I settle into married life than I started missing all the things I used to love. I should have been a single seventeen-year-old kid having a great time. Instead I was a seventeen-year-old married man with a family to support. Not only had I adopted Ruby's little girl, Diane, but pretty soon we had a son of our own. God knows, I don't regret that part. I just wish the circumstances could have been different.

Not surprisingly, I made one drastic mistake after another. Sometimes I had no idea what the consequences might be of seemingly the most innocent things, like naming my son Roy Linwood Clark II. Years later when he was all grown up, he wanted to take a stab at playing music. The trouble was, there was such a strong physical resemblance between us that any-time he applied for a job, for a driver's license even, he'd always be asked if he's any kin to *the* Roy Clark. For a while it was a very big hang-up for him, so much so that he eventually started using only the first part of his middle name, Lin Clark, to get away from the pressure of being Roy Clark's son.

Anyway, shortly after we were married, Ruby said she didn't want me playing music and hanging out at bars, even though she knew that was how I made my living. To try to please her, I took a stab at being a car hop in Bethesda, Maryland, right across the state line from the northwest section of D.C., where all the rich kids in their fathers' convertibles would come by with their tennis rackets and give me orders for food.

I hated everything about the job. I'd take an order from one kid, the second one would give me his, then the first one would change his order, and then so would the second one. I'd be standing there with my white, starched britches on, feeling like a fool, doing something I didn't want to be doing in the first place.

I worked there for about six months. The only good thing about the job was that I could make what to me at the time seemed like a lot of money. But I knew I had to get out of there. It wasn't that I was itching to go back to the club life. I was just itching not to do this, and the only other thing I knew was music. So I finally quit and went back to playing.

That's when my marriage really began to fall apart. Because Ruby didn't like what I was doing, I became rebellious and started staying out later and later, often all night. I'd play music from nine 'til two in the morning, then go find a place with four or five other guys and have a jam session. I'd think nothing of driving fifty miles if someone said there was a club owner who'd unlock his door and let us play for a while. So I started staying out and jamming all night, drinking, going out with other women, doing all the things that a kid should have been doing. An unmarried kid, that is.

Predictably, Ruby and I started having arguments, and then one morning in 1954, after about four years of married life, I came home one morning and found all my possessions sitting out on the lawn. That was the effective end of my marriage. I have to say in all honesty I felt no sadness about it. Rather, it seemed like a great burden had been lifted from my young shoulders. Now I was free to do the things I should have been doing, without always worrying if it was okay or not. In truth, Ruby and I should never have gotten married. It had been stupid of me, and she should have known better, too.

In the divorce settlement, she got the house, all the furniture, and our new Buick. I kept only my clothes and my instruments. It wasn't much of a house, but I kept up the payments on it, the car, and the furniture until everything was paid off. On top of that I gave her thirty dollars a week out of my earnings. To be honest, I would have agreed to anything to get out of the marriage.

The trouble was, I was only making about sixty dollars a week, and quickly realized I couldn't live on what was left for me, so after a while I had to cut back a little on her cash allowance. She promptly took me to court. The judge denied her any alimony but made up for it by cranking up the child support. Court appearances became a pattern. If we ever had any chance of keeping things friendly, hauling me to court for one thing or another for what seemed like every other week surely killed it.

I don't really know why, but back then, and still today, I have a tendency when something goes wrong to absorb the blame. As I look back on my first marriage I know I had a lot of faults and did a lot of bad things, but in my own defense I was just a kid, and never did anything maliciously. Nonetheless, Ruby filled the children with so much hate, it took years for my son and me to begin to get to really know one another. I wasn't allowed to visit a lot while he was growing up, and because of that I missed many special moments: his learning to walk, or to ride the bicycle I bought him, things like that. Ruby was so hostile about my seeing him or my adopted daughter, it was just easier for me to stay away. I figured when I left that it would be better for the children if she remarried right away, that it would be easier for them to have more of a normal life if I wasn't there, which was a bad mistake on my part. I figured if I couldn't be with them all the time, it was better if I wasn't with them at all. In that way maybe they could adjust to a situation where their father comes to see them on Sundays, but he's not really "father," because their mother tells them to call this other man "father . . ."

I'll never forget, after Ruby finally did remarry, I picked up Diane and Roy from Ruby's place and took them to my mother's for Christmas one year. Diane told me in the car on the way over that Ruby had filled them both with all these instructions, what to do, what not to do, and most of all, not to call me Daddy, that I wasn't their father, that Herb, her new husband, was their father. Diane was old enough so that she sort of understood, but Roy was still just a little guy, and didn't know who I was, or why he was there.

When they got to my mother's, we took Roy's snowsuit off, and he started running around the room. All of a sudden, out of the blue, he ran across the floor, and started staring at me. I was sitting in a chair as he ran up to me, opened my knees, walked right up to my face and said, "I know who you are."

"Oh? who am I," I said, real cheerful.

I thought he was going to say the Lone Ranger or somebody. Instead, he looked me right in the eye and said, "You're my father." I went, "Uuhhh . . . oohhh . . ." and wanted to get out of there. On his own, in that honest way kids have, he had just come up and told me what he felt.

One time a few years back he came out to visit me. We started talking and he said, "I've been trying to figure you out. The times I've been around you I cannot see all the bad things my mother said you were. It's confusing." Well, what could I say? I wasn't about to go into all those unpleasant things. I wasn't going to tell him his mother lied. It was a tough spot, and I just had to hold back. All I told him was that when we got to know each other he could make up his own mind. That's exactly what we did, and I'm real happy to be able to say there's a good feeling between us today.

I guess plunging back into music after the marriage fell apart helped me to survive it all. As I think about it now, I don't think I could have done anything else. Music has always been my survival, my way of life, although it took a while to understand just how important it really was, until one day, out of the blue, it hit me hard; in a single moment, a revelation that changed my life.

I was in my early twenties and had gotten totally away from sports. It wasn't just that I wished I could have been a baseball star, I *knew* I could have been, and I began to blame music for having kept me from becoming one. I'd left high school; I'd dropped out of sandlot; my marriage was over. The only thing I did now was play music, and because of it I was starting to get thick around the middle. One day I looked in the mirror, didn't like what I saw, and told myself if it wasn't for music I'd be in great shape. When I was sixteen, I had been a miniature dynamo. I never walked anywhere, I ran. I never got winded.

I never got sick, never even got so much as a headache. Now, still in my twenties, I was watching myself slowly start to deteriorate. A voice in my head kept saying, *"If it wasn't for music, I'd still be in great shape. Music has done this to me. Music is taking me away from what I really want to do."*

I remember looking at myself in the mirror one morning while I was shaving and hearing that same voice say, *"Look at that gut hanging out."* And then, just like that, I heard another voice. *"You ungrateful bastard. If it wasn't for music, you'd have nothing!"* My jaw dropped! There was no one else talking. No earthly person anyway. *"That's the only thing that sets you different. Music has given you all this attention, given you everything you have!"*

From that moment on, my attitude changed completely. I gained a new respect for my abilities. I suddenly realized that *in spite of myself,* music was my salvation, the thing I loved most and did best. Far from ruining me, it was offering the kind of life most folks only ever get to dream about.

That was the day I decided I wasn't going to be a dreamer, not about my life anyway. No sir. I was going to go out and live it.

Skull Orchards and a French Kiss at a Family Reunion

2

In 1950, at the age of seventeen, just before I got married, I won the USA Country Banjo Championship, a five-string banjo contest held in Warrenton, Virginia. First prize was five hundred dollars cash and a chance to perform at the Grand Ole Opry. Even though without question this was a great career opportunity for me, I had mixed emotions about going to Nashville. I was living in a little apartment I shared with two other musicians, just down the street from my parents' home. Except for that brief two-week stint I had done for Connie B. Gay when I was fourteen, and the summer I spent playing at North Beach, this would be my first trip away from home for any real length of time, away from everything and everyone I knew and loved. I had become quite comfortable with all the work I was getting in clubs, on local radio and television, and wasn't sure I wanted to change anything.

Ralph Case, who was to prove so fundamentally important to my early career, insisted I couldn't afford *not* to go to Nashville. He kept telling me, "It'll be one of the biggest breaks of your career." Ralph not only convinced me to go but drove me to the station and bought my bus ticket. Just before I left he shook my hand, looked me straight in the eye, and said, "Now you go down there and do good."

For a while, it seemed I might never actually get the chance. The trip from Washington, D.C., to Nashville took two days, and for some reason I never figured out, the bus wound up in Kentucky! When we got to the state line I was instructed to get off and board another bus, which took me to yet another destination, and yet another bus. For two days, I remember doing nothing but changing buses every hundred miles or so, riding and changing, riding and changing, in very hot and uncomfortable conditions. What made it even worse was that I was traveling with a cardboard suitcase held together by a piece of rope, my brand new Fender guitar I bought with the money I won from the contest, and my banjo. Every time one of the buses came to a stop, even if it was only for a rest, I had to take everything out of the rack and off the bus with me, because they wouldn't check musical instruments underneath with the other luggage.

When I finally did arrive in Nashville, I got off the bus and hadn't taken more than two steps before I was greeted by A. V. Bamford, one of the judges of the contest who also happened to be a promoter in Nashville. Bamford drove me straight downtown to the lobby of the building that housed radio station WSM, and introduced me to two legendary Nashville acts, Lonzo and Oscar, and Stringbean. We then all got into a car and immediately left on a two-week tour of eastern Colorado, Texas, and Oklahoma. I had been in Nashville for all of forty-five minutes before I found myself right back on the road again!

Lonzo and Oscar were top of the line acts, as was Stringbean, and they were all advertised as such. I was billed at the bottom as "Extra Added Attraction: Musical Wizard Roy Clark." We went out for two weeks playing theaters so small, as Grandpa Jones used to say, "you could take a bow on stage and shake dandruff in the lobby." That small. We played these little neighborhood theaters Monday, Tuesday, Wednesday, and Thursday. Fridays, we'd team up with a major country star, either Ernest Tubb or Red Foley, and play a gig in a larger city. Afterwards they would continue on to wherever they were going—Nashville, or maybe a big dance in Texas—while we headed back for the regular Saturday night performance at the Opry.

I had to keep the look of awe off my face, because out of the chute I was playing with the biggest stars, right up there with country music performers who were my heroes. Not only that, but I was being paid more money than ever before, by far. I earned five hundred dollars in cash for those first two weeks alone.

When the tour ended, Bamford offered to let me stay at his house in Nashville, out on Franklin Road. I guess he felt I was too young to stay by myself in a hotel, which I had never done. In exchange, for room and board, I did small chores for him, like going to the store, driving his wife someplace, or taking the car to get serviced.

I actually played at the Opry one or two Saturday nights. Not headlining or anything, mind you, mostly just backup work for Lonzo and Oscar, but still rubbing elbows with legends; talking, listening, watching Lefty Frizzell over here warming up to go on stage, all the great pickers over there, some of them sitting right next to me in the dressing room, jamming, playing jazz and just swappin'.

Talk about a heady atmosphere! Every great name I'd ever

heard in my life was literally brushing up against me. I had the same feeling a country boy gets going to the big county fair, only instead of looking at all the lights, I was privileged to look at all the stars. And I'm sure I stared at every one of them. The best thing about it all was that when I went to bed at night, I'd wake up the next day and all of this would continue.

I'd been in Nashville for about six months when I started getting these pains in my stomach. I didn't know it, but I had begun to develop an ulcer. The pain became so bad, it got to where nothing would appease it. I couldn't eat anything except milk, white bread, and baking soda. I'd be walking down the street in Nashville and the pain would come on so bad I would fall into a doorway and double up. I'd have to take my fingers and gouge myself in the stomach until it let up enough so I could go on. I decided to leave Nashville because of the ulcer, and also because I had become really homesick, having been able to go home only once, at Christmas.

Back in Washington, doctors X-rayed my stomach and confirmed that I had a duodenal ulcer in the first passage of the intestines. I couldn't understand why. I wasn't drinking a lot, the food I was eating was greasy, which would irritate an ulcer once you have it, but wouldn't cause one to develop. My dad had an ulcerated stomach and the doctors suggested I might have inherited the condition, but that theory has never been proved. After a while, I began to think it might have been related to homesickness. They say the emotions can affect one's health, and, hey, I thought I was living proof of that.

Whatever the reason, the doctors prescribed all these powders for me to take before meals, and drops of stuff in water to drink after. The ulcer lasted eight years, from 1952 to 1960, coming and going, although it was never as intense as it had been when it first flared up.

In spite of my illness, I felt great about being back home with my friends and especially my family, every one of whom I'd missed so much. The only person from home I'd seen regularly was Ruby. We had gotten serious enough for her to come and visit me in Nashville, prior to our getting married.

I was now some sort of local hero. *I had been to Nashville, Tennessee!* That experience gave me the kind of credentials I needed to get work in real nightclubs, as opposed to the skull orchards, toilets, and dives I'd played before I left. The nicest among them were the Bob White Club, the Famous, and the Dixie Pig.

Now, to play the Dixie Pig, that was the epitome, especially with that barbecue drive-in right next to it! I got booked into the Dixie Pig for a hundred and fifty dollars a week, whereas before I had gone to Nashville, the most I might make in a week at any D.C. club was maybe eighty-five dollars.

Remember, I was no longer just another one of the guys playing in bars. I had *done* things. I was a *professional musician.* I had something to sell now, something the club owners could put in their newspaper ads. *"Direct from Nashville, Tennessee! Roy Clark appearing tonight and every night!"* It gave me enough of an edge so that for quite a while if there were two performers they were considering hiring, they would always choose me.

Something else had changed as well. For the first time in my career, I was performing solo. Carl Lukat and I had worked as a team since we met in 1948, and continued until he was drafted late in 1951, shortly before I left for Nashville. We had been playing in a little club called the Campus, a motorcycle hangout right on the District line, when he got his induction notice.

After I returned from Nashville, one of the clubs I worked at for a time was the Famous. Mickey Woodward of the Woodward Brothers asked me to fill in for his brother, Roger, who had joined the navy. When Roger returned, the two brothers bought a club of their own in Georgetown, the Shamrock, and left me behind at the Famous where I stayed on as a solo act.

I'll never forget when Carl came back from the army. Before he left, we had talked a lot about how when he came back we would continue performing as a team. Now I was working on my own at the Famous, honing my act, developing my songs, and just starting to add a little comedy into the mix, when one night while I was on stage, doing my thing, out of the corner of my eye, I saw Carl sitting right down front. I figured he must have stepped off the train and come right down to see me because he was still in uniform.

After my set, we sat and had a beer together. We chatted for a bit, and then he suddenly looked up and said, "Roy, you really learned a lot since I last saw you." There was a tear in his eye when he added, "There's no room in your life for me now. You've gone so much further than me." Then he slapped his knee and said, "You're great!"

I didn't see much of Carl after that, except for one time when he came to see me at another club where I was playing. After, we went to his apartment. He had bought a new guitar and wanted to show it to me. He hit a couple of licks on it, then put it down and we spent the rest of the night talking and drinking.

That was the last I ever saw of him. A couple of years later, I heard that he and his girlfriend were pulling out of a restaurant down on highway 301 when a car hit them broadside and killed them both.

Carl was an important early influence on me. He was a great guy and the first lead guitarist I ever knew, and he taught me a lot, not only about music, but about life. He was like a big brother to me, and I'll never forget him.

For a musician in the early fifties, Washington, D.C., was the place to be. The town was an amalgam of different music and cultures from all over the world, which made it a great proving ground for someone like me.

The cultural sophistication, coupled with the lure of life in the nation's capital attracted young people from all over the country. Women right out of high school came to D.C. hoping to work for the federal government as secretaries and assistants, "girl-type" jobs, as they called them back then. With so many young soldiers stationed in and around Washington, a terrific social scene developed. As much as Hollywood was the center of motion pictures, and Nashville country music's recording capital, D.C. was where the club scene blossomed. The District was very bar oriented. Almost every block had a neighborhood bar or club that offered some sort of live music. At its peak there must have been upwards of 150, 200 clubs in operation. They were always packed, and every night seemed like Saturday night.

The Famous, the Shamrock, Harry's Tavern, Strick's, the Dixie Pig, all the better clubs had individual personalities, and strong loyal followings. The same faces always showed up. Working those clubs was the greatest education somebody in the music business could have.

As with any scene, there were local rules and regulations that nobody quite understood. In D.C.'s case they actually helped the club scene expand, by pushing it outward to the neighboring states. Because of local ordinances, you could get a beer or a glass of wine at a D.C. bar, but you had to be seated at a table to get whiskey. If you were meeting people, you had to sit at the bar and wait for them to arrive. When they did and you got a table, you could not take your beer with you. A waitress had to deliver it. Nor could you stand or leave your table with a drink in your hand and go to the bar.

The clubs could stay open until two in the morning, which meant the music had to stop by one thirty, the latest twenty 'til two. Saturdays, the biggest night of the week, the mandatory closing time was twelve. On Sunday only beer or wine could be sold.

At the same time, just over the city limits, Maryland's liquor laws were wide open, which resulted in a lot of after-hours clubs, on both sides of the state/District borderline. These clubs really thrived on Saturday nights, especially because of the District's mandatory early closing time. The after-hours clubs were all illegal, which meant you had to bring your own bottle, and the clientele was mostly black. The only way you knew how to find one was by the so-called underground word of mouth. It was in these clubs that I started playing with black groups. Around midnight, everybody would head over to one of those places, and party until five in the morning. They were forever being busted, which was the reason why they had new locations all the time.

There were some great musicians who played the club circuit in those days. I remember a "fast" guitar player from Pennsylvania named Al Alexander. He never became a name, but he wrote a song I recorded and sometimes still do in my show, "Drifter's Polka." Al was the first "fast" guitar player I ever heard. Boy, he could just blaze all up and down the neck of that guitar. He intrigued me and I guess that's what got me leaning toward trying to play fast and speedy things.

There was another guitar player, an older man from Arkansas by the name of Bill Harrel. Bill, who was the fellow that had taken my dad and me to meet Al Alexander while we were still playing square dances together, was a "pop" guitar player. He was the first person to show me how to make barred chords, and taught me how to play "Slow Boat to China" that way. He was very influential in my guitar education.

Mostly, though, my style of playing country evolved from basic hillbilly string music, à la Roy Acuff, influenced, because of D.C.'s cosmopolitan mix, by jazz, pop, and early rock and roll. To that end I've often wondered what my musical tastes would have been like, and where I would be now, if I had been raised in Meherrin, Virginia. Moving to Washington at a young age and being inspired by all these other musicians and a variety of sounds greatly influenced my preferences in music and the way I play it.

I spent ten years in bars around Washington, D.C., ten years of a special type of schooling I could not have gotten anywhere else. D.C. is where I learned to play before live audiences, and where I really developed my comedy *schtick,* the foundation for my becoming a professional country music performer.

A lot of people may not realize it, but back then, parts of D.C. were very "country." To us, the urban Capitol Hill community in the northwest section was a world away. We occupied the southeast, southwest, and northeast sections, where there was a very strong southern feel, and a very large black community. Back then, everything was very segregated, except music, which is why a lot of country music was so influenced by early black blues.

In the late forties, early fifties, D.C.'s music scene got so big it began to attract performers from all over. Among the many who passed through, I remember Charlie Daniels performing in D.C. in the late fifties. He called his band Charlie Daniels and the Jaguars, and they had a hit rock and roll instrumental, "Jaguar." He wore black horn-rimmed glasses, a blue blazer, a thin black tie, and black slacks, and did those white rock and roll moves, à la Bill Haley and the Comets.

The first time I met Charlie, we both happened to be working in a place called Stricks. Every Sunday, there'd be a battle of the bands type thing. My band would start at one o'clock in the afternoon and alternate with Charlie Daniels and the Jaguars all night long until closing. We did that for several months.

The next thing I know, Charlie Daniels is having hit records. Years later, I happened to run into him at one of the big music industry functions at the Grand Ole Opry in Nashville. Into my dressing room walks Charlie Daniels as everyone knows him today, husky, with that big cowboy hat pulled down over his eyes. I said, "Hey, Charlie, it's great to see you! Boy, I can't believe how long it's been!" He just looked at me and said, "Yeah, good to see you. I got to go. See you 'round." It was almost as if he didn't want to be reminded of that "other" Charlie Daniels.

Maybe one reason is because back in the fifties, you couldn't give country music records away. To survive, a lot of country artists had to "cross over." Marty Robbins was one who did and he had a big hit with "A White Sport Coat." Sonny James was another, with "Young Love." Marty Robbins, Faron Young, and a lot of others all changed their tune to fit the times. Instead of cowboy shirts with the fringes, and boots, they suddenly started wearing cardigan sweaters and loafers to sell records.

Hey, I did it too. Rock and roll was just beginning to happen, and the people coming to the clubs wanted to see it performed. I did all the early Buddy Holly, Bill Haley, Fats Domino, and Little Richard tunes. Actually, I found it kind of funny when I discovered that if you put a heavy backbeat on a Hank Williams record, it sounded just like rock and roll. Even Elvis's first records were nothing but country tunes with a backbeat.

I performed all the hit songs in my act, regardless if they were pop, rock and roll, or old standards, including "Sentimental Journey," "Perfidia," "Twilight Time." If the audience wanted to hear them, I played them. I did everything, with about sixty percent of country rolled into the mix.

Given the kind of high energy scene D.C. was, I suppose it's inevitable that the energy sometimes turned a little negative. Like any nightside scene, we had our fair share of brawls. To be truthful, for years I was scared to death of that side of the business. Although I'd boxed, and felt I could take care of myself, I still saw some nasty, terrible, mind-boggling brawls. I saw eyeballs laid out on a guy's cheek. I saw people hit in the face with a full beer bottle. I always thought, well, I don't have a beautiful face, but I don't want to be up there in the spotlight with scars all over it and no teeth.

So I backed down from fights. And boy, afterwards it really bothered me. Somebody would get up in my face, and broken bottles and dangling eyeballs would flash in my mind. It would drive me crazy. I'd get in the car and actually break down in tears on the way home, furious at myself for acting like a chicken.

This went on for years, until one day, to prove to myself I wasn't a coward, I started to look for a fight. All the abuse I'd taken, all the times I'd backed down, now I wanted to look at a guy and say, "So what's wrong with you?"

I didn't have to look very far. There was always somebody to take me up. Now I was going home every night with my clothes nearly torn off my body and my hands busted and bleeding. Thankfully, I got over this period in my life when I realized one day that God had given me these hands to make music, not to fight drunks. Once I passed that corner, I found a new sense of peace in myself, and playing became even more fun than before.

So there I was, a young, single guy having a ball. I was making good money playing the clubs every night; my pockets were filled with cash. Ruby and I had separated, I had lots of girlfriends, and, best of all, no responsibilities. Every night the pretty girls would come by, usually in twos without dates, and take a table. Sometimes four or five servicemen would come in and sit at the table next to them, and before long they'd all be together. Other times I went after them myself.

There was a kid in my band by the name of Tommy Johnson who played steel guitar, a real nice-looking guy, and he knew it. Tommy and I would sit on stage playing, until it was about eleven, when probably all who were going to be there that night had arrived. Then we'd start making our choices. We'd always go together, looking for double-dates. When we'd settle on two that we liked, we'd take an intermission and Tommy would go over to them and say something like, "Hi, how y'all? Roy and I would like to buy you a drink," and most times they'd say sure. We'd usually home in on the ones we had been eyeballing from the stage with cute little winks.

Of course, sometimes things didn't work out the way we planned. Occasionally, we made our choices a little too soon. The first two would be nice enough, or we wouldn't have been over there, but then, every so often, ten minutes after we bought them that first drink, and things were getting friendly, two real scorchers would hit the door. That's why we always tried to wait until eleven o'clock!

I guess I was always a bit of a natural clown. In school I could make my classmates laugh. I still love to see people laugh. Part of the reason why, both then and now, I think, has to do with self-confidence. I'm not overloaded with it even to this day, probably because of my limited education and my lack of formal musical training. Humor has always provided me with a good cover for these shortcomings.

In the early days, I always felt intimidated whenever a really good guitar player would come around, thinking that since I wasn't as good as he was, maybe I wasn't good enough to be there. I would always want just to drift back into the wood-work. But then I found that by acting the fool on stage I could effectively mask my lack of self-confidence. They say someone who doesn't have a lot of self-confidence is the first to laugh out loud and make a joke, because he wants to be the first one to laugh at himself. If I did something on stage and it got a laugh, I kept it in as part of my regular routine.

I never sat down and wrote or rehearsed any dialogue, or planned anything out. A lot of my "garbage," as I like to call it, came out of everyday conversation, corny jokes, a combination of stories I'd heard other people tell. To this day, most of the *schtick* I do happens because silence on stage scares me to death. I want something happening all the time. I'm afraid if I don't keep it going, someone in the audience will start talking back, "Hey, Clark, what do you think you're doin' up there?"

For years, there was a fellow around Washington by the name of Billy Strickland. I had heard about him long before I started playing the club circuit. They called him the King of the Hillbillies. Billy had a double-necked steel guitar up on high legs that he played standing up, unlike most steel guitar players, who sit down. He had a Fender or Gibson with no strings on the inner neck where he liked to set his drinks and rest his elbows, like it was a desk top. The thing about Billy was that in an hour's set he might play one, maybe two tunes. The rest of the time he spent talking.

He would say and do anything. He cussed on stage, which was a strict no-no back then, but he did it anyway. People talked about him as being "dirty," but very funny, and there's always an element that goes for that kind of humor. He played the choicest places, drew the biggest crowds, and I have to say I learned an awful lot from him about how to "work" an audience for the most laughs.

Through the years, I discovered how comedy can be the greatest release there is, which is why I'm grateful for the ability to take certain serious difficult situations and make them seem easy. For instance, if someone is sitting in the audience, depressed, blue, or maybe with a bad sickness, and I can cause him to laugh, I've always felt that's a real accomplishment.

In addition to playing the clubs, I began doing a lot of local radio and making occasional television appearances, although nothing on a regular basis. I also started doing some recording.

A man named Ben Adelman owned a little studio in Washington on the far side of town. I don't recall how I met him or how I got up there, except I do remember when the word went out along the boulevard he was looking to record anybody and everybody in town who played country music. Ben had a deal with a California-based fellow named Bill McCall, who owned a label called Four Star. Ben would ship all his recorded tapes to Bill, who would then put them out on record.

Ben's studio was on the top floor of a narrow, old two-story building. When I say studio, I mean it in the loosest sense. Although he eventually did upgrade his equipment, when I started recording with him back in 1951, his operation was little more than an empty space with lots of outlets for plugging in amplifiers, a microphone, and a tape recorder. There was no mixing or anything like that. You simply positioned yourself as close to the mike as you wanted to be, depending on how loud you were going to play. Your performance was taped and that was it; what you put down was what you got back. If it was a step up from home recording, it was only because there were no babies crying in the background.

In those days the kick came in hearing yourself being played back over the studio monitors and saying, "Is that what I really sound like?" Or if you were really lucky, you'd hear yourself on the radio. That was really the only "pay" that counted.

Because Ben recorded just about everybody, he wound up with some tapes by people who became big stars, performers like Patsy Cline and Jimmy Dean. Oftentimes, these artists forgot they ever made recordings for Ben, until years later when they would turn up, bad sound, mistakes and all, on various $1.98 compilation albums.

I know because it happened to me. A recording I made for Ben Adelman, intended for Four Star, wound up instead on Coral Records. Although I'd never met anybody from Coral, and never signed any contract with them, one day years later I discovered I had a record out on that label.

Sometimes Bill McCall would send songs published by Four Star to Ben Adelman and ask to have them recorded. Adelman would then get, say, Roy Clark to record a particular song, and not say anything to Jimmy Dean about it; then he'd have Jimmy Dean record it and not tell Roy Clark. That way, Adelman and McCall might get as many as six recordings of the same song. Adelman could then approach a big label and say, "I have a record here of 'Release Me' by Roy Clark. You want it?" If they passed on me, he could follow up with, "Well, how about the same song by Jimmy Dean?" That's why, even though I did the first or second cut on "Release Me," it eventually became a big hit for Ray Price. Later Engelbert Humperdinck also had a hit with it, while my version was never released.

The way I found out about this game was one night while I was playing at the Famous, during a break a waitress came over and said, "Patsy Cline's on the phone." I picked up the receiver and said hello to Patsy, who then asked if I had recorded a certain song. I said yes, and asked her how she knew. "Because," she said, "Ben just gave it to me to learn, and wants me to record it."

Well, I was devastated. I almost broke down and cried right there on the phone. When I finally got my composure, I said, "Hey, that's the way it goes, I don't mind, Patsy, you go ahead and record it."

She said, "No, I don't play that way. It didn't have your name on the label or anything, but I knew it was you. I don't play that game. If they want somebody else to record the song, fine, but old Patsy ain't doin' it."

Patsy Cline was one great lady. She didn't owe me anything, but she wasn't going to hurt me by playing Ben's game.

I began recording just about the time Jimmy Dean asked me to join his band, the Texas Wildcats, which consisted of Jimmy on accordion and a little piano, Marvin Carrol on steel guitar, Herbie Jones on rhythm, and Buck Ryan, one of the top fiddle players on the East Coast. Both Jimmy and I had been recording for Ben, and that's how we really first got to know each other. I often played guitar on Jimmy's records and he played piano on one or two of mine, sometimes in the same day.

Jimmy was from Texas, and his music was heavily influenced by Bob Wills's swing sound. At the same time Jimmy was trying to establish something unique on his own. He also had the gift of gab, which helped him enormously. He was personable, charming, and could sell you anything, including the fact he could sing! In his later years, I think his salesmanship actually overshadowed his music. When Jimmy left the band in the early sixties to go solo and recorded "Big Bad John," that's when Herbie Jones said, "If Jimmy was ever going to have a hit record, he'd have to have talked his way through it, 'cause he can't sing all that good!"

While still in the air force, Jimmy, who'd been stationed at Bolling Field, started playing the local D.C. club scene. After his discharge, he married a local girl and took a job working in Dub Howington's band, the Tennessee Haymakers. Dub was a terrific guitarist, and a major influence on me. When Dub was drafted, Jimmy became the leader of what eventually became the Texas Wildcats.

Jimmy called me one day in 1954 and said, "Come on, Roy, I really want you to join the band. We're doing a six-day-a-week radio show over WARL, in Arlington, Virginia, and getting ready to add a five-day-a-week local television show."

I said, "Well, how much will you pay me?" He offered me a hundred dollars a week. I said I couldn't afford to do it for that, I was already making a hundred and twenty with my own "band," which was really nothing more formal than a bunch of guys I had begun playing with on a regular basis.

Jimmy said, "Well, let me call Connie." Connie B. Gay, the same promoter who had booked me in Baltimore, was now managing Jimmy. That same afternoon he called back and offered me a hundred and fifty dollars.

I spent two years as a member of Jimmy's Texas Wildcats, during which time I learned a great deal about the music business. Among other things I learned how success wasn't a hit-or-miss thing, but something that had to be planned from day one. Jimmy was a great example to me of how far commitment and determination could carry you. He was absolutely determined to make it. While the rest of us would play the scheduled gig, then go out and jam the rest of the night, drink, and maybe get up a poker game, Jimmy would head straight home and go right to bed. The next morning he'd be up bright and early, calling people. He went so far as to take Dale Carnegie courses to improve his presentation.

Jimmy Dean's was the first organization that opened my eyes to the idea that music was a *business,* and, as with any business, success doesn't just "happen." The gents in dark suits don't just walk in from Hollywood or New York and say,

"You're just what I've been looking for, sign here, take this check and let's go."

Jimmy's was the first band I ever worked with that actually had a manager, Connie B. Gay, who was always after us to think of ourselves as professionals. Legend has it that Connie began his career selling five cent potato peelers on street-corners for a quarter apiece. From that humble start he eventually became President Roosevelt's Assistant Secretary of Agriculture, and after the war remained in the D.C. area, got into radio, became one of Washington's top disk jockeys, and eventually moved into personal management.

Connie ran everything for the band. We knew where to show up every night and every day, we knew where we were going a week from Monday, what time, and for how much.

We did a lot of free functions for Connie, who often booked us to play at political rallies and barbecues for politicians, where everyone would be dressed in blue jeans with kerchiefs around their necks for a "hillbilly day." They were about as exciting to me as French kisses at a family reunion.

Jimmy, however, would always make it a point to get to know the politicians. I might say, "Hi, how you doin' " to them, but Jimmy would get to know them, as if he might be able to use this fellow somewhere down the line. It was always, "Let's keep in touch," that sort of thing.

I joined Jimmy just as the group began the six-day-a-week radio show on WARL that broadcast from eleven to quarter of twelve every morning. We had to be at the station early every morning to work on the show. Before we went on the air, we would sit down and write everything out.

In addition to the radio job on six, and sometimes seven nights a week, we played a lot of dances, and all the better

clubs. Once or twice a week we played a place called Waldrops, a supper club out on Rhode Island Avenue. Waldrops
was definitely one of the bigger and nicer clubs around.

The band also did a two-week tour of Philadelphia, Baltimore, Washington, and Richmond, Virginia, with Ernest Tubb,
Red Foley, and Andy Griffith. Andy did skits as the Reverend
Andy Griffith, and the band became part of the skit. As a result,
Andy and I became good friends. He was originally a music
teacher at the University of North Carolina when he started
making comedy records, parodies of *Romeo and Juliet,* and
Swan Lake. I enjoyed his sense of humor, he liked mine, and,
as I say, we just hit it right off. Almost every night, after the
show, we'd go out to get a hamburger and shoot the breeze.
One night he told us about an experience he had just before
the tour in New York, where he'd gone to read for a part in a
new play. "If I get it," he told me, "it'll make me a star."

The play was *No Time for Sergeants.* I remember when the
tour ended and he went back to New York, he called Jimmy
and me on the phone, screaming, "I got it, I got it . . ." He did
the play first on live television, for the "The U.S. Steel Hour."
Then he appeared in it on Broadway and eventually starred in
the movie.

Coincidentally, about ten years later they were going to
make a TV series out of *No Time for Sergeants,* and I was one
of the people called to New York to read for its producer, the
legendary Sam Goldwyn. After my audition, he looked at me
and said, "You're interesting, but you haven't got it." He gave
me some pointers and another scene to read. He told me this
version of the Will Stockdale character was going to be different from the one Andy Griffith had created, more of a country
bumpkin, always messing up, without Andy's redemptive in-
nocence and charm.

I studied the new scene for two days, went back and read for Goldwyn again. I'll never forget, he sat in a swivel chair behind his desk and spun around so he couldn't see me. He wanted to hear if the character came through. When I was through, he turned around with a smile on his face and said, "I believe you've got it. Now I want you to go out to California and read for Jack Webb."

At the time, Jack Webb, the same Jack Webb who produced and starred in the "Dragnet" TV series, was the head of television development for 20th Century-Fox. I waited in his outer office for a considerable period of time, then was led into the inner office and made to wait again, which I guess was part of the protocol. When Webb was finally ready, he called me in, took one look at me and said, "You're too fat. Nice to have met you." That was it, I was out the door, just like that. Welcome to Hollywood, Mr. Clark!

Anyway, Jimmy's band had been playing Waldrops every Tuesday for about a month when a local meat packing company named Briggs offered to sponsor us on television. Jimmy had been doing their commercials on the radio program, and they liked the way he made it sound as if he were talking one-on-one to the housewives. As I said, Jimmy knew where he was going from day one. He was no ordinary accordion player who sang country songs. No sir. This boy knew how to take care of business.

The television show debuted on a Monday night in the fall of 1954. These were still the early days of live TV and we played fast and loose. It didn't take us long to start pulling tricks on each other. The control booth was on the second level, and tilted, so you could see the people inside as they looked down at the studio. They'd count us down—you know, four, three, two, one—and give us the go-ahead. One time Jimmy told us beforehand, just lip-synch but don't make any noise. Up in the control room we could see the engineers frantically grabbing knobs, waving their arms, figuring something must have gone wrong with the audio. Finally, we started laughing and went into the theme.

We also did a televised square dance every Saturday night that was picked up by several stations in northern Virginia and Pennsylvania. On his way through Washington one time, Colonel Tom Parker came by with Elvis Presley to pay a call on Connie B. Gay and arrange for the band to back up Elvis on a gig. Talk about a laid-back country boy. All "Yessir," and "Thank you very much." I saw him again later on when he came out of the service. Elvis was always a big television watcher and when we ran into each other he made a point of telling me how much he loved "Hee Haw." I think that at heart he was really a frustrated guitar player. At one time he wanted to learn how to play it, but then his voice took off, he became a big star, and no longer had time to practice and really get into it. But if you've ever seen his 1968 "comeback" TV special, you know he could lay claim to a few licks.

I remember at the time we backed up Elvis, the Colonel was trying to sell Presley's contract to Connie. Parker wanted something like eight million dollars, and he was willing to take it in payments over time. Connie told the colonel, "I think he's great but I don't think he's got a future."

After the Colonel left, Connie told me that Parker said that I really had it. In fact, Connie said, Parker's advice was to forget about the tall guy with the accordion and stick with the guitar player; he was your future.

We did the TV show five nights a week, from 7 to 7:30, on ABC's District affiliate, WMAL. We would all arrive at the studio by six, make up a loose schedule, go to makeup, and do the show. Usually, after our regular evening broadcast, we would have to literally run out of the studio, jump into our cars, and drive to another engagement, sometimes as far as a hundred miles away. I'd usually get home by one or two o'clock in the morning, wake up early the next day, and start the same thing all over again.

Waldrops, where we did our regular Tuesday night gig, normally held three hundred or four hundred people, and while our weekly appearance had developed a bit of a following, we weren't exactly setting the world on fire. We usually had half-audiences, sometimes a quarter-house, which for a weeknight wasn't all that bad. Our first TV show was broadcast that Monday evening. Then, at the end of our regular seven o'clock airing on Tuesday, Jimmy announced the band would be appearing at Waldrops later on that night. We all headed out to the club, and found to our amazement traffic was so backed up we had trouble even getting near the place. The television show had made us hotter than a depot stove! After being on the air for about a month, every place we played was the same, packed with people, with hundreds more outside not able to get in.

I met my second and present wife, Barbara, at Waldrops. She was a secretary back then, and had come to the club with a group of friends to celebrate a birthday by going out to see "the hillbillies."

Barbara was born and raised in Maryland, had two children,

and was separated from her husband when we met. She'd left home and gotten married at a very young age, primarily to get away from a very domineering father. Later on they became very close, but at the time he was very strict. He had three daughters and a son, and the girls really had to toe the line.

Well, this one night I was on stage when she walked into Waldrops. I looked down and saw her pretty, warm smile, and just . . . well, you see now, *that* was *love at first sight!* *BANG!*

I just had to talk to her! I flirted with her from the stage for about an hour, and I think Barbara thought I was a bit of an idiot. I was supposed to be in the background, playing guitar, when the next thing I know I'm pushing Jimmy aside, playing all these hot licks and rolling my eyes around trying to look real cute. I was bashful, and one-on-one wasn't really my style. I was usually too scared for it, but that night a bigger lust just overtook me.

When our set was done I finally got up the courage to go over and ask her to dance. Now, you can count on your fingers and toes the times up until then I'd danced in my life. Barbara tells the story about how my cowboy boots ruined her shoes and nearly cut the hose off her legs! She says by the end of the dance her shins were bruised, her hose was hanging down her feet, and my toes kept catching her about the knees while I was high-stepping. I mean, I was all over her! I thought I was Fred Astaire, so, so *SWAAYYVVE!*

Somehow I managed to get her phone number. I called her the next day and invited her to come back to the club the following Tuesday, and she did, with her friends again. She had recently gotten separated and my marriage had just ended, so I guess we were both naturally a little cautious.

Here I am at age 3, in New York.

2

3

1

Mama and Daddy holding me as a baby
in Fairpoint, Ohio, in 1934.

Hester Clark (my dad) and
Kenneth Clark (my uncle).

Here's a school picture of me in Meherrin, VA.

4

5

6

My version of a singing cowboy, when I was in fighting shape!

That's me in the front row on the extreme right.

7

On my St. James motorcycle in Meherrin, VA, in 1946.

1949. From left to right: Speedy Tolliver, Cy Kines, a couple of the other boys, and Carl Lukat, next to me.

8

Washington, DC, 1949. Left to right: Curley Irvin, me, and Smitty Irvin.

10

9

The Camden Tavern in 1949. Left to right: me, Buster Austin, and Pete Pike.

Carl Lukat on Yuma Street, S.E., Washington, DC, in 1949.

11

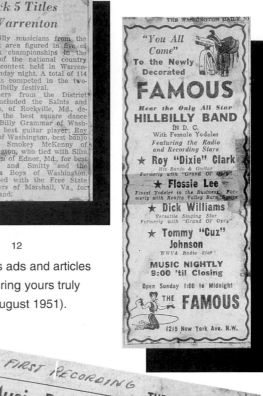

12

Various ads and articles
featuring yours truly
(August 1951).

13

Billboard magazine review of
my first recording, "Sugar-Coated
Sweetheart," 1951, and a picture
of me in Nashville at the Grand
Ole Opry, same year.

At the Famous in Wash-
ington, DC, in 1952
with Mickey Woodward.

14

15

16

Again at the Famous in Washington, DC, 1952.
Me, Mickey Woodward in the middle,
and Roger Woodward on the right.

Picking a banjo at a
picnic in northern
Virginia in 1951.

The Covered Wagon in Washington, DC, in 1952 with Wade Holmes to the left of me and Richard Johnson to my right.

17

18

The Dixie Pig in Bladensburg, MD, in 1952. Standing, left to right: Blackie Skiles, Stoney Rigsby, Smitty Smith, Chubby Wise, Jimmy Burkett;

That's me in a blond wig singing the girl's part in a duet with Mickey at the Dixie Pig in Bladensburg, MD, in 1953. Left to right: Mickey Woodward, Stoney Rigsby, and me.

19

That's me in 1954 on the tree stump with Jimmy Dean and the Texas Wildcats.

20

21

Country Music Contest

National
Championship
Country
Music
Contest

This certifies that

ROY CLARK

is awarded second place for

BANJO PICKER

in the

NATIONAL FINALS
WARRENTON, VIRGINIA
August 7, 1955

President, Warrenton Jaycees

Master of Ceremonies

Me at First
Street, S.E., in
Washington, DC,
in 1955.

22

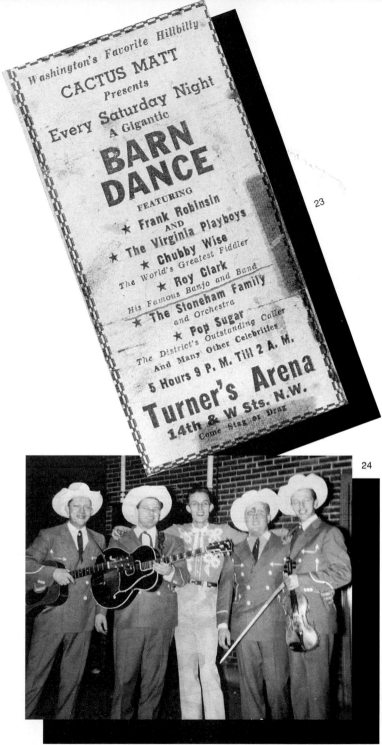

23

24

Jimmy Dean and the Texas Wildcats, 1955, at the
National Guard Armory, for the "Home Show."

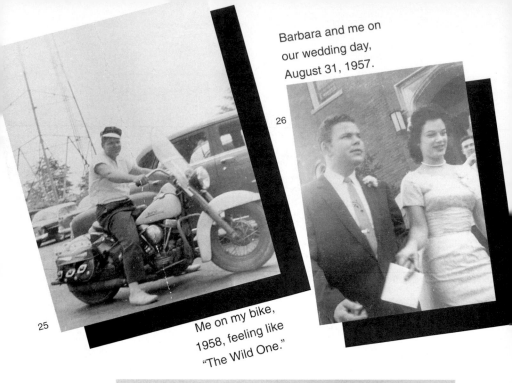

Barbara and me on
our wedding day,
August 31, 1957.

26

Me on my bike,
1958, feeling like
"The Wild One."

25

Here I am
in 1958.

27

28

With Jimmy on "The Jimmy Dean Show" in 1967.

Wanda Jackson and me at the Golden Nugget, Las Vegas, in 1960.

29

30

A marquee
for one
of my
Las Vegas
appearances.

JIM HALSEY PRESENTS
FRONTIER COUNTRY MUSIC FESTIVAL

Roy CLARK
AL ALVAREZ ORCHESTRA

LYNN
ANDERSON

MAY 26-29   MAY 30   JUNE 12
FREDDY FENDER   M-M-M MEL TILLIS
GEORGE "GOOBER" LINDSEY   CARL PERKINS

ROOMS NOW AVAILABLE
ALL SPORTS TV CHANNEL

Eddy Arnold presented me with the Entertainer of the Year Award at the Country Music Association Awards Show in 1973.

32

Barbara and me with June Carter and Johnny Cash at the 1974 Country Music Association Awards Show in Nashville.

Barbara and me in Las Vegas in 1975. Our "home" was courtesy of the Frontier Hotel where I was working.

33

Here I am with Marie Osmond, Cheryl Tiegs, and Tammy Wynette during the filming of my 1977 special.

34

Here I am on my 1976 tour of the USSR.

35

I started calling her a lot after that. I found it very easy to talk to her. Conversation just flowed. Among the many fun things we discovered was that when I was fifteen my dad and I had played a dance for the VFW in Cheverly, Maryland, that she had attended. That meant she had actually first seen me when we were both only fifteen.

It wasn't long after Barbara's second night at Waldrops that we started dating. However, because she lived in Tuxedo, Maryland, over the District line, and I was working these long hours, we weren't able to get together that often.

What we did do was talk over the phone an awful lot. I'd call her in the morning before the radio show, then again after. I had a block of free time between the radio show and the television show, and I'd always spend it on the telephone with Barbara.

It's a funny thing about this business. Musicians don't do a lot of "date" dating, as in, I'll pick you up at eight, we'll go to dinner and the theater. Most of the time it's, "Why don't you come down to the club where I'll be playing tonight." You get to smooch awhile and then take your "date" home. "I'd like to go to the movies tomorrow night but I can't. I'm working." Or, "I'd like to take you to dinner but I can't. Why don't you come down to see me play, and after, we'll go grab a bite to eat." That's more or less the extent of the single club musician's social life.

I believe that's why there's so much marital trouble in the entertainment business. In order to be successful, the entertainer has to be totally committed to his career. The spouse who isn't performing usually winds up, consciously or unconsciously, having to make all the sacrifices, and all the concessions. There's just no half way.

Barbara and I were married on August 31, 1957. We had to wait that long until both our divorces became finalized. I had already moved into her parents' house, with her mother and dad and sisters. They built an enclosure around a porch area and made a living area out of it, which I rented from them.

About forty people attended our wedding. My dad filmed the whole thing with his movie camera, and both Barbara and I looked as if we were going right to the gas chamber, that's how scared we were. It was as if the preacher said to us, "I now condemn you to death!" After all, we were both coming out of unhappy, traumatic marital experiences. Neither of us had completely healed from those wounds, and here we were flinging ourselves right back into the emotional thick of it. Though we knew in our hearts we were doing the right thing, it was still pretty scary.

We moved to nearby Hyattsville, Maryland, into a basic, middle-income one-bedroom apartment. We didn't have a lot of money, just enough to buy what we needed to furnish the apartment on time. One thing we did buy was cemetery lots! And we still have them, in Fort Lincoln Cemetery, right outside of Washington. Her mother and dad also bought plots there, as did my sister, her husband, her brother and his wife. The Clark clan owns a couple hundred acres in that cemetery, and believe me, some good arguments have developed because of it! "I don't want to be here if he's going to be there." "I don't like her husband, so put him over there . . ." *Oh boy!*

After the wedding, I continued working with Jimmy's band, playing the clubs, the local radio and television shows, regional fairs, and fire halls. Fire halls were very big back then. Every volunteer fire department in town had a weekly carnival and we wound up playing a lot of them.

Barbara took a job as a secretary at the local Harley-Davidson outlet, which was great for me because it meant I could get parts for my Harley at cost. Because we didn't have a car, I would take Barbara to work every day. She would sit side-saddle on the motorcycle, all dressed to the nines, a nice tight, form-fitting skirt, blouse, and high heels, with her hair all done up. She'd wrap a little scarf around her head, and we'd take off.

Looking back, I have to say we were having a great fun time. There were no real pressures, very few responsibilities, nothing hanging over our heads. Like a lot of our friends, we lived from payday to payday, making just enough to meet our needs, with nothing left over. Both of us were working very tough schedules, and loving every minute of it.

Between our radio, TV, and club dates I was with Jimmy and the band from early morning until early the following morning, with very little time off. If we were due to open somewhere at seven o'clock, and I knew it took thirty minutes to get there, I would leave twenty-five minutes before and trust that every light would be green, there'd be no traffic, and I'd make it. I've been that way my whole life, and because of it I've always been late.

My problem with punctuality eventually became a major bone of contention between Jimmy and me. He started getting on me for being late, and my excuse was always the same. "Hey, Jimmy, I'm here, ready to go, let's do the show!" But he would dwell on it. He was so organized and so professional he just refused to put up with it. The final blowout came one day when Barbara and I decided to take a motorcycle ride very late on a Saturday night, out through the countryside. The band was due to open an appliance warehouse the next morning at eleven, one of those typical gigs, designed to bring people in to listen to the music, while everything in the warehouse—freezers, refrigerators, and air-conditioners—is on sale.

Well, I got a flat tire. I found a farmhouse nearby and called a wrecker. When he arrived, the mechanic chained up the bike and took it about thirty miles to the service station.

We had to take the saddle bags off, the fender, the chain, the wheel, the tire, the tube, patch the tube, put everything back, and realign the tire. By now I was full of mud and grease. Unless you're in a motorcycle shop, which we weren't, a flat tire on a bike is a much more complicated affair than it is on a car, and it wound up taking all night.

By the time we got back home, cleaned up, and arrived at the warehouse, it was a quarter after eleven Sunday morning, and the band was already playing on a makeshift platform. I came wheeling into the backstage area, ran up, and found my instruments all sitting there waiting for me. When Jimmy saw me, he said, quietly but with a note of determined finality, "Don't bother taking your guitar out of the case. You're through."

"Hey, Jimmy, come on," I said, and reached for my instrument.

"I told you, Clark," he said. "You can play all you want now, but you're through." And he meant it. After the set he told me, "Clark, there's no doubt in my mind you're going to be one of the biggest stars in country music. But right now I just can't afford you. I can't afford someone who is not more reliable."

Connie tried his best to get us back together. After the show, Jimmy was flying to Nashville for a recording session, and Connie flew down with him. Before he left he called me and said, "Just cool it, don't cause any arguments, any hard feelings, and I'll talk to Jimmy." Later on Connie told me he talked to

Jimmy all the way down and all the way back, and but before they landed on the return trip, Jimmy said, "Well, Connie, I'll tell you. It's this way. It's either him or me."

Jimmy went on to host CBS's national morning show, opposite "The Today Show" on NBC, and for a while actually drew bigger ratings than Dave Garroway. I, meanwhile, went back to doing what I had been doing before I joined the band. I put a couple of guys together, and we played the club scene, along with lot of local television and radio.

I did one TV show called "Cactus Mat's Big Red Barn." Cactus Mat was a character invented by the local news anchor, Mathew Warren, a very serious, deep-voiced, "Good Evening, Ladies and Gentleman," kind of anchor, who, when he became Cactus Mat suddenly was all, "Hya there, neighbors, how y'all doin'?" It was his impression of the kind of music a lot of us took quite seriously, although its very name—hillbilly—seemed to conjure up condescending images of the worst kind.

I had always played, in one variation or another, what is, essentially, hillbilly music. I don't think many of the performers objected to the term "hillbilly," but the promoters and managers, the business side, were finding it increasingly hard to overcome that automatic look down the nose. Up north, in New York City especially, where the music business was centered, "hillbilly" wasn't a term used with a lot of love.

"I have Jimmy Dean down in Washington . . ."

"Oh you mean that hillbilly act down there?" Now, Jimmy wasn't averse to saying he played hillbilly music, either. Hey, that's really what we were—hillbilly performers. Still, there were those who preferred calling hillbilly something with a little more class. That's when hillbilly became "country western," instead of just country, or western.

To me, hillbilly butted one end right up against Jimmy's main stylistic influence, Bob Wills and western swing, and the other end against my main influence, your basic Roy Acuff. I've never been ashamed of or embarrassed by saying I'm a hillbilly singer. On the contrary, to me, hillbilly is authentic American music, and I've always been extremely proud to play it.

Still, it was a very hard sell on the national scene, and, like a lot of others, I tried to give different audiences what they wanted. Just before Barbara and I got married, thanks to Marvin Rainwater I got a chance to appear on "Arthur Godfrey's Talent Scouts." Marvin was a country artist heavily influenced by Hank Williams. I knew Marvin from appearing at the Famous, where he would often get up and sing Hank Williams tunes with Mickey Woodward and me. When Hank Williams died, Marvin recorded a tribute to him, "Life's Hall of Fame." It was that song that got him on the Godfrey show. Whoever was the weekly winner then became a guest for the following week on the Arthur Godfrey weekday morning TV show. Not only did Marvin win, but Godfrey liked him so much he kept him on the morning show for three weeks.

Ray Rainwater, Marvin's brother, was a very successful landscape contractor who wanted to be a manager. One day he sold his business and decided to concentrate all his time and effort on managing. He heard me perform, and said he wanted to try to get me on Godfrey. Sure enough, he worked it out so I could go to New York and audition.

Barbara and I moved up to New Jersey where Ray lived, and stayed with him while he set up the audition. In the meantime, he booked me into all these little places around Elizabeth, Roselle Park, and other New Jersey towns, in what they called "cowboy bars," where they played what they thought sounded like country music.

Finally, I took the audition, passed, and, sure enough, was booked to appear on the Godfrey show in the spring of 1957. The way it worked, you came out and performed, then they brought you back to do a little encore as the audience voted with its applause for its favorite.

The song I chose to do was Carl Perkins's "Blue Suede Shoes," which, although Carl had had the regional hit, Elvis had taken it national with his rock and roll version. Of all the songs I'd suggested to the producers, they decided that was the least offensive. Actually, my first choice had been "Long Tall Sally," but they said the censors would never allow that song, which I thought was pretty funny, since at the time it had been a huge hit for Little Richard and was still being played on every jukebox and radio station in the country.

I finally, and somewhat reluctantly, settled on "Blue Suede Shoes," precisely because rock and roll was so hot. I figured I had a better shot doing that than anything hillbilly in front of this New York audience. I wore a light blue sport coat and a tie for the occasion, and, hey, *I had moves!* I didn't wiggle or jiggle like Elvis, but I did move in time with the music's rhythm.

My chief competition was an opera singer, and I have to say she was really great. When it was time for the voting, the needle that measured the applause went almost all the way over for me and stayed there. I thought I'd won for sure. Then the opera singer came out, the needle went *bam!* all the way over, and came all the way back, and Godfrey declared her the winner.

Even though I didn't win, just being on Godfrey's "Talent Scouts," one of the biggest shows of its time, meant a lot to a newcomer's career. Now, club owners who booked me could advertise, "Come see Roy Clark! You saw him last week on the Arthur Godfrey Show!" In fact, right after my appearance, Ray got me a booking in Boston for two weeks, in a club called the Show Bar, where, I must say, I didn't quite fit in.

The main room had a big, beautiful mahogany bar that surrounded the stage where all the acts performed. Besides me, there was a chorus line of girls, an orchestra, a comic, and a boy singer, "light in his loafers," who sang "On the Street Where You Live."

We didn't exactly shake up the world those two weeks. More to the point, we left Boston literally dead broke. The Godfrey show hadn't paid anything, and all the money I made at the Show Bar went to pay for a room at a boarding house.

As soon as we arrived home, I decided against any further excursions outside my loop. I put a new band together and went to work at the Dixie Pig, filling in for two weeks for another act, and wherever else I could hustle a night or two to tide me over until I got myself working once more for Connie B. Gay, and indirectly, with Jimmy Dean.

Jimmy was doing his early morning show out of Washington, D.C.'s, CBS affiliate, WTOP. Because this was in the day before videotape, Jimmy had to do two forty-five-minute broadcasts every day, one for the East Coast and one for the West. In between they'd break for an hour or two. Connie negotiated with WTOP to fill the local fifteen minutes following Jimmy's network forty-five with my band and a kid from Delaware named Johnny Linden. So Jimmy and I wound up sharing the hour time slot, with both shows produced by Connie B. Gay.

To get the CBS morning show, Jimmy had to give up his local evening TV show, because it was on the competing ABC affiliate. Connie replaced him with Grandpa Jones and used my new band to back him up. Connie owned that time slot, as well as the local fill for Jimmy's CBS network show. Connie liked me, thought I was talented, and used me as much as he could.

About a year later, he brought George Hamilton IV up from North Carolina, and started actively promoting him. Just around this time, Connie and Dean had a falling out and split up. What caused it I don't know but it was very bitter. Connie was philosophical about it, however, and Jimmy wasn't. You could always talk to Connie about Jimmy, but you could never talk to Jimmy about Connie. Connie then finagled a deal with ABC for a network summer replacement show out of Washington, D.C., starring George Hamilton IV. One night when I was playing the Dixie Pig, Connie called and told me he was going to do this new network television show and that he wanted me to be a regular on it.

I remember when we went on the air we were panned by the New York critics—how dare a network television show come from anywhere but New York City! One writer said the show looked like it was filmed in a phone booth. Maybe so, but we had some great talent on, and that summer I was all over the tube.

But I wasn't kidding myself. My popularity, such as it was, didn't extend beyond the local D.C. area. I had played every place, every function, from teas to square dances. I even played the White House one time in the early fifties when my dad and

I went there with Ralph Case to teach Margaret Truman how to square dance.

And I continued to appear on local television, even when I finally found that regular gig I'd been looking for. Also in 1957, I became part of the Shamrock Trio, along with Mickey and Roger Woodward. It was during this time at the Shamrock that I really developed, refined, and polished my act.

We would start playing at nine o'clock every night, do a forty-minute set, then take a twenty-minute intermission. Most of the time I'd take the first intermission. Then, for the rest of the night, until ten minutes 'til two, I wouldn't leave that stage. During every intermission that followed I'd stay up there, kibitzing with the audience, doing all kinds of nutty stuff. Sometimes Mickey or Roger would join me, we'd put on wigs, do boy-girl duets, I'd be the girl . . . I mean we got far out.

Mickey kept a can of lighter fluid near the volume foot pedal of his steel guitar. The pedal had a tendency to pick up dust and get scratchy, and lighter fluid worked great as a cleaning substance. Well, one night we were flying, I'd taken a lot of Dexedrine, and he squirted my whole head with the lighter fluid and was looking for a match. The only thing that saved me was he couldn't find one! He joked to me later he would have definitely set me on fire.

I should say right here that back then, Dexedrine, or "uppers," as we called them, was a way of life for musicians. We took them as casually as people who get up in the morning and have to have a cup of coffee. Nobody knew about the dangers, the way we do today. Being a little heavyset, it was easy for me to go to a doctor and say, hey, I want to lose some weight, can you give me some Dexedrine. For a time it became a way of life. I would get up, take a pill, and then maybe have a little something to eat. I'd have coffee, the caffeine would kick in, and I'd be ready to go for the day.

I was always careful not to overdo it. Not because I was intelligent or smarter than anyone else, just a little more scared. I feared if one of those little pills could make my heart beat faster, what would three do, make it explode? All I wanted was to feel like I thought I should be feeling if I was in good health and well rested. I didn't want to get high, I just wanted to get by.

Since then, of course, pills like that have been made illegal, and rightly so. It probably sounds like a crutch and a cop-out, but back in those days everybody in the business did it. You had to be up, alert, funny, good, even if you didn't feel well, even if you had a cold or a headache, even if you just found out your mother had fallen down and broken her arm. People in the audience paid their money to have a good time, not to know your problems, and they were absolutely right about that.

Drinking, too, has always been a problem for country performers. So many get into it simply because they play a lot of bars. Or, a guy's working on the farm slopping hogs, feeding chickens, he goes in, makes a record, it's a smash, he's taken immediately out of that one environment and put into another, which he doesn't know anything about. He's scared to death, he's had no training, no rehearsal for the move, and he can't handle it. So he finds, very early, that a few drinks out of the bottle will supply all the courage he needs. Well, that few drinks will lead to a few more drinks, until there's no way he can go on stage without it. Now he has a problem.

There's a classic story about Hank Williams and his notorious drinking habit that finally got him fired from the Grand

Ole Opry. He used to go on stage smashed, unable to stand, and still the audiences loved him! Because of that he almost ruined a lot of careers. One night, Ray Price went on drunk, and afterwards the Opry management went to his dressing room and told him he would not be allowed back on stage in that condition. Ray Price supposedly said, "Hank Williams does it!"

Management's answer? "Well, son, you're no Hank Williams!"

As I said earlier, I did my share of drinking, but never on stage. My daddy told me when I first started playing clubs, "You remember, if you ever get to the point where you have to get drunk to play good, you'll be the only one who thinks you're playing good." That stuck with me from day one, along with something else I learned early on. As drunk as somebody is in the audience, they don't want to see another drunk on stage.

As my act developed, I realized about eighty-five percent of it was off-the-cuff comedy. If I happened to say something funny, I'd try to remember it and keep it in the act. I never bought a joke from anyone. Minnie Pearl is the greatest in life at telling the same old jokes and making them sound like it was the first time she's ever thought of them. To me a "funny joke" is like a hit record. People will bring other people to hear the joke, and if you don't tell it, they'll say, I brought my friend all the way from so-and-so and you didn't tell the one about . . . !

I started doing a lot of song parodies in my act. One time a fellow came into the club and asked me to sing one of them

"Eli Presswood" records. That immediately became a part of my act. I used to come out and say, in my best Elvis voice, "I have a little tune here originally cut by Eli Presswood, and to do it right I have to put my guitar down." I'd slip the strap off, put it down low and try to play it down there. Then I'd say, "That's funny, I got the guitar down where it belongs and now I can't see it." And I'd go *bbbb . . . bbb . . . bbbbabbeee . . .*

I also did Fats Domino. Fats was hotter than blue blazes back then. Very stylized, very easy. Then maybe a takeoff on the "Rock Island Line." There was a trolley, the M Street line, that ran past the club, crossed the District line into Virginia, made a circle, and came back into Washington. One night, I came out and started singing, "Now this here's the story about the M Street line. The M Street Line is a souped-up converted street-car that cruises down M Street . . ." and so on.

I parodied the Platter's "The Great Pretender," doing all the voices and all the sounds. That came about because it seemed every time we took a break that same song came on the juke-box. When I would return to the stage, people would shout out for me to do "The Great Pretender." One time I said, " 'The Great Pretender' is four people, and a full orchestra, and you want me to do it? All right, I will." Then I named all the instruments on the record, and threw in a harp, a glockenspiel, and even a guy in a corner keepin' time on soup spoons. I said I loved the song but couldn't afford all of that. "Instead, what you're about to hear is me doing the song and fillin' it in myself. Even the little guy in the corner with the soup spoons." Which is exactly what I did!

I began to develop quite a reputation as a cut-up. People started coming to the club not only to hear me sing, but to see this crazy guy. They came looking for a yahoo time, and, boy,

I gave it to them. I don't think the kind of rapport I had with those audiences really exists anymore. These were the golden years of nightclubs, during the infancy of television, when clubs and bars were an integral part of people's social lives.

I've always been a showman, always had fun with my music *and* my audiences, which probably has more to do with my success than any other single factor. I guess it goes back to something Louis Armstrong once said. Someone asked him, "Louis, do you read music?" and he said, "Not enough to hurt my playing." I don't read at all either, but I have tried to develop a style that's fun, and not above a lot of people's heads. That's why those years I played the clubs in D.C. were so important to my development. I played from nine o'clock to two o'clock in the morning, seven nights a week plus a matinee. I had the time to keep my chops up, and to learn while I was doing it, because I wasn't under that critical spotlight. I was free to experiment, and that was where the real excitement was for me. I don't think I've ever played as well as I did in those days, nor was I ever as funny.

I was probably making, with the kitty and everything, two hundred fifty, maybe three hundred dollars week. I didn't have a whole lot, but I didn't need a whole lot. I was like a country kid who goes to the county fair and is totally blown away watching the Ferris wheel going around. Up to then his life has been plowing, gardening, milking, feeding hogs, and stuff, and suddenly he's standing barefoot watching this big wheel with lots of lights on it going 'round and 'round.

Once he's gotten the nerve to ride that wheel, he wants to know what else there is that he's been missing. He wants to see a bigger town, meet a prettier girl, have a harder drink of liquor. The more he sees, the more he wants to see. Like the good ol' boy once said, how you gonna keep 'em down on the farm after they've seen the farm!

Well, my first Ferris wheel of lights had just let me off, and the midway pointed toward another, bigger fairground just up the road, a little farm they called Las Vegas.

The Turning Point

3

By this time I had been playing the D.C. club circuit for nearly ten years, and had become something of a fixture on local radio and television. I had performed at every type of function imaginable in and around Washington. I was probably very well known within a three hundred mile radius of D.C., but a virtual unknown everywhere else. One day I looked around and realized that a lot of my friends who were still playing in clubs were fifty-five, sixty years old, with no savings in the bank and not a penny in their pockets. These poor souls were destined to play clubs until the day came when they were too old even to climb on stage. They had no security, no health benefits, no medical coverage, nothing. As the fifties came to a close, I promised myself that no matter what, I wasn't going to wind up like them.

Just about this time, one of the great female country stars, Wanda Jackson, came to play the Washington area. Wanda was more than just a great singer, she was an inspiration to a whole generation of singers. Brenda Lee and Tanya Tucker are just two among the many whose style has been influenced by her.

Wanda was really hot in 1960, having had several very big hit records in a row, including "Let's Have a Party," "Fujiyama Mama," and "Right or Wrong." In addition, she had just been signed to open at the Golden Nugget, the "in" place for country music in Las Vegas, where all the biggest names played. Part of the deal was that Wanda had to bring her own band, which at the time she didn't have. She was also looking for a front man, somebody who could do emcee work, one of the reasons she'd come to D.C.

Some mutual friends of ours, girls I'd met during my years with Jimmy Dean who had also become friends with Wanda, brought her down to the club where I was working to see me perform. The next day Wanda called up to say she was getting ready to go to Vegas, and wanted to know if I was interested in coming along.

There was no question it was a great opportunity for me. It also forced me to make a big decision. Barbara and I sat down and talked about whether or not I should do it. We talked that night about a lot of things: my fears about the future, about how in ten years no big talent scout had come along and offered me a hundred million dollars because he thought I was so great, about how I was a little older now, twenty-seven, and running ever faster just to keep in place, about how maybe there were no real opportunities left for me in Washington, about how I might be able to make a deal with another nightclub for ten dollars more a week and work there until another club owner offered me five dollars more than that, while, in reality, I'd still be working for nothing. Now, suddenly, a real opportunity had suddenly come along—the chance to work with a really big star in Las Vegas!

By the time dawn broke, Barbara and I agreed I had no

choice—I had to take the offer. We both understood there was no long-term financial security for us if I continued to play the D.C. clubs, and that this was an opportunity for me to make a career move. Although she wasn't totally happy about my leaving, Barbara remained totally supportive. That meant a lot to me. I wouldn't have taken the job if she had asked me not to.

To reassure her, I said something like how I would probably be gone for only a month, two at the most, knowing full well in the back of my mind that if things worked out it might in fact be a year or two before I came home. We did agree, though, that no matter what, we wouldn't stay apart for long.

I had my share of apprehension about leaving. After all, I was saying goodbye to an area and a situation in which I had become quite comfortable. My home, my family, and all my friends were in Washington. I knew my way around D.C., and as a performer had built a pretty good following. And here I was about to give it all up for people and places unknown.

Making matters even worse was that some of the guys in my band got angry because I was making my move without them. A couple of them waved their hands at me and said, "Aw, you'll be back with your tail between your legs in a week." I told them maybe so, but I was still going. I didn't blame them for reacting the way they did. So very few musicians who ever left Washington actually "made it." Most who did leave came back sooner than later and these boys assumed that I would, too.

Just after the first of the year, I packed up my car and headed west. Barbara and I had been living alone—my kids were with my first wife, and Barbara's were with her husband's mother and dad—so when I took off, she decided to keep herself as busy as possible. Barbara took a job in Washington at the Gaslight, a club modeled after a classy twenties speakeasy, where, in addition to serving drinks, she performed in skits dressed as a flapper, and generally added to the atmosphere of the club.

I drove to Oklahoma City, where I met up with Wanda and the other members of the new band she had put together. I left my car there and drove the rest of the way with Wanda, her dad, Tom Jackson, and her manager, Jim Halsey, in her brand new Cadillac. Halsey had decided to come along to smooth over any rough edges and to provide moral support for his star.

The rest of the band shared a car and a trailer, which also carried all our equipment and instruments. For the next month, to break everyone in, we played a lot of dances and clubs on a little minitour Halsey put together on the way to Vegas. Included were stops in Lubbock and Odessa, Texas, and Grant and Albuquerque, New Mexico. This was all very new and exciting for me. The farthest west I had ever been was when I had first gone to Nashville in 1950, and the tour I had gone out on that played eastern Colorado, Texas, and Oklahoma.

When we finally arrived in Las Vegas, that glorious, glittering oasis in the desert proved to be everything I imagined it would be, and a whole lot more. The Golden Nugget seemed like country heaven, with three or four heavy-duty country acts rotating with two lesser acts all day and most of the night.

Unlike a lot of the other hotels, the Golden Nugget didn't have a separate, "main room" theater. Instead, everyone played in an open lounge, which was freely available to anybody who wanted to come by, sit, have a drink, and listen for a while. This was a pretty good arrangement, except for one thing. There was always a problem with management about the music being too loud for the gamblers. We kept getting called down about that, which always struck me as being funny. My whole life I had worked to get audiences to loosen up and have a good time. Now, these unsmiling casino pit bosses in too-tight suits were complaining about all the racket we were making. It was as if they wanted us to be good, but not that good!

During Wanda's engagement, we shared the bill with such country greats as Bob Wills, Hank Thompson, Hank Penny, and Jimmy Wakely. The way it worked was, the headliners, including Wanda, performed from nine o'clock in the evening until two in the morning, on a forty-twenty set-up, meaning the star did forty minutes with his or her band, followed by a twenty-minute break. The lesser acts, our band included, coheadlined the eight to nine hour, then filled in the off hours between eleven at night and seven the next morning.

One night a week every headliner was required to work "the swing." This meant the band would do a show at seven and again at eight, followed by a two-hour break. Wanda would then come on at nine, do two shows back to back, then we would come back and do two more shows, finishing at three in the morning. Also one night a week everyone had to do a "graveyard" shift. That meant showing up at two in the morning, and getting off at seven, followed by almost two complete days off.

It was my job to open for Wanda. I'd come out and do a twenty-minute "Roy Clark Show," with the band backing me up. After the opening I'd bring Wanda out to complete our forty-minute set. Besides singing, I did all my comedy *schtick,* the same material I had developed back in Washington, and I have to say I always tore the place up. I may not have been all that great a talent, but I was different! In addition to playing and singing all the standards, I did my parodies, I sang with an empty water glass turned over on the mike stand, which I then used as a slide against the guitar strings, a crazy way of playing bottleneck style. I even played the guitar with my feet! I can say with all confidence these audiences had never seen anything like what I did. I had real chops from my ten years in D. C. I could play six hours every night, then go and hang out with a bunch of guys and jam until after daylight the next morning. Sometimes I'd find a group of boys and wind up playing blues and light jazz until it was time to break for breakfast.

I also discovered a lot of nonmusical things in Las Vegas, among them the many games of chance that kept those glittering casinos filled with people. Wanda's father, Tom Jackson, had tried to warn me about them before we arrived—the games, not the people. "Now, when you get out there," he said to me on the way, "you're going to want to gamble, because everybody does."

I said, "Well, not me."

"You don't play cards?"

"Sure," I said, "I play cards, but I don't gamble." I explained to him the only cards I played was a little poker with the boys in the bands back in Washington, usually with a quarter limit.

He smiled and said, "You'll gamble."

Sure enough, my very first night in Las Vegas, I strolled through a casino, and eventually found myself behind a 21 table, learning the game by watching others play it. Before very long I started saying to myself, oh, that dummy, he doesn't understand anything about this game! The next thing I knew I felt my hand in my pocket groping for my money as I looked at the cards, thinking I had it all figured out. Then I looked down and saw I'd pulled a twenty out of my pocket. I put it back in, and left the casino.

The second night was a different story. I quickly blew that first twenty, and the twenty behind it, just like that! I was like that good ol' boy and his wife sitting at the 21 table. He turns to her and says, "Honey, where's that twenty dollars I told you not to give me? I need it, honey . . ."

I was bitten by the bug and, like every gambler, thought I could control it. The only reason I can even talk about what happened to me now is to remind myself what idiots we all can be at times. It finally caught up with me years later, when I was making fifty thousand dollars a week in Reno, and *lost fifty thousand dollars playing Blackjack in one night.* When I told my accountant, he said I had to make three times that amount to cover it. That cured me of gambling, just like that. *Whooaa, no more cards for this old boy.*

My association with Wanda Jackson proved the turning point in my career. That first gig at the Golden Nugget lasted four weeks, after which the band continued on with her and played Milwaukee, Minneapolis, and several record hops set up for Wanda by her record label, Capitol Records. In the fall of 1960, I went with her to Nashville to play guitar on her album *There's a Party Goin' On,* as well as on a couple of singles.

It was still considered unusual for Capitol to record artists in Nashville, at the old Columbia Quonset hut's famed studio 10, rather than in the modern Capitol Tower in Hollywood. Another "first" was that Wanda was allowed to use her own band, augmented with Nashville session pickers, rather than established studio players, which is how I managed to play on her albums.

At the time, Ken Nelson was the head of Capitol's country music division. He had been with the label almost from the beginning, and when Capitol decided to start a country division, they had asked Ken to run it. He came down to Nashville while Wanda was recording her album, and during a break he asked me how I'd like to record for Capitol on my own. I said, "Whooa, I'd love it." I didn't bother to ask "How much do I get to sign?" Nor did I ask what my royalties would be. I didn't ask anything. All I could think to say was, "I'd love it; when do I start?"

"The thing of it is," Nelson said, "I know you like to sing, but I won't be able to sign you as a singer. I'll have to bring you onto the label as an instrumentalist. We have so many singers, if I go back to Capitol and tell them I've signed another vocalist the top of the tower might blow off. However, I can sign you as an instrumentalist. I'll work you in that way, and eventually you'll get to sing some songs."

"Fine," I said.

Perhaps the most important thing to come out of my affiliation with Wanda Jackson was meeting Jim Halsey, the legendary country music manager, someone I've now been professionally associated with for more than thirty years, a man I'm proud to call my friend.

Jim was born and raised in Independence, Kansas, the home of Sinclair Oil. Independence was strategically centered between Kansas City, St. Louis, and Chicago. Back in the touring days of the big bands, Independence became the stopover of choice for the big bands to play on their way to the major dates. Because of that, many of the biggest stars in the world headlined there.

As a boy, Halsey played saxophone in the high school band, and for a time thought about maybe becoming a performer himself. He likes to tell the story about how when all these acts came to town, there was always a big black Cadillac parked at the curb, and a band bus in the back behind the building. He once asked the chauffeur who the car belonged to, and the driver said the band's promoter. That's when Halsey realized performers rode in old raggedy buses, while promoters rode in limousines.

Tall Hog at the Trough

4

When I finished my engagement in Las Vegas, in January of 1961, Jim Halsey had arranged for me to start touring the country. The plan was that I would open in Charlie Genova's Chestnut Inn, in Kansas City, a club I had first played with Wanda Jackson. Charlie, like Bill Green of the Golden Nugget, had gone to Halsey and told him he wanted to have me back, even without Wanda. That was why Halsey chose his club to open the tour.

In the interim, Barbara and I drove out to Los Angeles, where I had originally intended to meet with some of the executives at Capitol Records. Because Halsey had now taken over those negotiations, I found myself with a few open weeks before my gig at the Chestnut Inn. So Barbara and I decided to return to Washington. The trouble was, we were so broke, my dad had to mail me his gasoline credit card, and we had to borrow food money from Barbara's mother.

We had been staying with some friends out in Los Angeles, and just before we began the long drive back east, Barbara started getting these bad pains in her stomach. When they didn't let up she went to a doctor, who gave her a quick examination and prescribed some pain pills. Although we were scheduled to leave the next day, the doctor told us he thought it would be best if we stayed in Los Angeles until he could find out what was causing those pains.

Well, the pills seemed to work, and because we didn't know when we would get another chance to go home, we decided to head out as scheduled. We started the drive and before long, the pain returned, worse than before.

Meanwhile, I put on a burst and drove nonstop halfway across the country, from Los Angeles all the way to just outside of Arkansas. Finally, when I was exhausted and couldn't go a mile farther, I pulled over to the side of the road. "Honey," I said, "can you drive for a while? If I can close my eyes for thirty minutes I'll be all right." Barbara said fine.

As soon as I hit the passenger seat I went out. Barbara drove about five miles before she woke me up, crying, with tears streaming down her face. She was literally doubled over in pain. I knew then that something was seriously wrong, so I took the wheel, drove to the next service station, and asked the attendant where the nearest hospital was. He directed me to Conway, Arkansas.

I headed straight for it as fast as I could, but by the time we arrived at the emergency ward, Barbara could no longer straighten up. The intensity of the pain had caused her muscles to contract and she was curled up in a fetal position. The nurses put her in a wheelchair, took her in and a doctor by the name of Fred Gordy immediately examined her. I could tell from the worried look on his face that something was very wrong.

He sat me down, and as calmly as he could told me Barbara

was bleeding internally and had been for a long time, which was what had been causing her so much pain. Then he hit me with the really bad news. "I need your permission to operate and we can't linger. I've got to go in right now, open her up, try to fix what's wrong, close her up and pray."

Needless to say, I told him to do what he had to. As tired as I was, I didn't get a second's sleep as I waited for hours outside the operating room. When he finally emerged, Dr. Gordy came over to me and said softly, "She got through it."

He then explained to me that Barbara had suffered a tubular pregnancy. Ironically, what had caused the pain and the bleeding was also what saved her life. Usually in a tubular pregnancy, he said, rather than traveling to the uterus, the egg lodges in one of the Fallopian tubes, and eventually bursts. When that happens, it's all over. They can't save the patient, not even in a hospital, because she'll lose blood too quickly. In Barbara's case, what saved her was that instead of rupturing, her tube had split, and blood oozed out just slowly enough so it could be discovered and repaired in time.

Or so we hoped. All I could do now was continue to pray. Dr. Gordy told me there was nothing more I could do there, and sent me up the road to a little motel. I checked in, went to my room, and crashed.

When I awoke, hours later, I jumped out of bed and ran right back to the hospital, where I waited all day, before returning to the motel to get more sleep. Three days passed before we knew for sure Barbara was going to pull through, and even then, she was in for a long recovery. I had no work and no money, and since there was nothing else I could do there, I decided it might be best if I continued the trip back to Maryland by myself. I went in to say goodbye to Barbara, who was still only semiconscious, and explained what I was about to do. She smiled faintly and groaned.

All I can say is there really are some fantastic people in this world. God bless Dr. Gordy and the people who worked at that hospital. They all took such great care of Barbara. They put her into a semiprivate room, and all the nurses and staff just really made a special thing out of her. They did their best to make her feel very much wanted, cared for, and perhaps most important, loved.

When she was finally well enough to leave, I wired her the money for a plane ticket. Some staffers of the hospital drove her from Conway, Arkansas, to Little Rock and stayed with her until she was seated on the airplane.

I've yet to get a bill from Dr. Gordy or the hospital. When we hear about doctors today, so much of the time it has to do with greed, overcharging, the high cost of medicine, and all of that. Well, Dr. Gordy and his staff are one shining example of what we don't hear about nearly enough—dedicated healers who are also good and decent folk.

My highly anticipated opening at the Chestnut Club in Kansas City was marred by a terrible snowstorm that threatened to close down the entire city. In spite of the weather, that first night the club was packed with people who remembered me from when I had played there with Wanda, and were willing to brave the elements to see me again.

It turned out to be a terrific engagement for me, and as I was finishing up my two weeks, Jim Halsey arranged to introduce me to Hap Peeples, one of the Midwest's legendary country music promoters. Hap ran a very popular package-show circuit that usually offered two headliners, a Ray Price and maybe a

Jim Reeves, backed by three lesser-known supporting acts. His tours always started in Kansas City, and traveled through Joplin, Sioux City, Sioux Falls, Lincoln, Topeka, Salinas, ending up in Wichita.

Halsey had called Hap and told him about me. Hap said, "I really don't have any room left on this next tour."

"Well," Halsey said, "let me bring him over on Sunday, let him do a couple of songs and see what you think." That's the day they did three shows, one at two, one at five, and one at eight. To most musicians the longest day in life in Kansas City is working a Hap Peeples show at Memorial Auditorium on a Sunday.

I went over and did the shows, had a great response, and Hap said, "Well, I don't have any room on the tour, but I'll make some for Roy!" He offered me fifty dollars a day plus transportation.

I was set to begin the day after I finished at Charlie Genova's. Barbara put all our furniture in storage, took everything else we owned, squeezed it in our 1957 Ford station wagon and drove out to meet me back in Kansas City, where I returned after the tour ended.

We then went out together on the road for the next 345 days, without a break, going wherever Halsey told me to. While I was away with Hap, Halsey had called all the places I had worked with Wanda and asked, how'd you like to book Roy Clark? Oh yeah, they'd say, he did great here, sure, book him.

Most nights, Barbara and I checked into the cheapest motel we could find. She would then drop me off at whatever club I was playing, and while I rehearsed with the house band, she would return to the room and sleep. When I finished performing that night, she'd pick me up and we'd get right back on the road to the next gig. The only time I was able to sleep was during these long stretches, upright in the passenger's side of the car.

I would sleep that way while she drove, until she would get tired, then we'd switch places and I would drive while she slept. If we didn't have to go too far I might be able to catch a couple of hours of rest in a motel. Then Barbara would sleep again while I went to the next club and the whole thing would start all over. Sometimes we drove as much as nine hundred miles in a stretch, traveling all night, and arrive at the next gig just in time for me to start rehearsing.

I was making four, maybe five hundred dollars per week, working seven nights a week. However, more important to Barbara and me than the money was the fact that we were sharing an adventure together, what we called our little crusade toward a better future for both of us. Sometimes, though, the adventure outweighed the togetherness. One time we drove up to Minot, North Dakota, where I was scheduled to start a two-week mini-tour that would take us through Canada. As we rounded the hill into Minot, the rear end fell off the car. I had to leave Barbara behind to get the car fixed. Luckily, we knew some people there who took her in, while I went ahead and finished the tour.

For the most part, though, it was great fun. Whenever we returned to a club I had played before, we would have friends there, and we'd know the house band. Sometimes for the occasion they'd bring their wives along, and if Barbara wasn't too tired, she'd come, too.

We lived this way from 1961 until 1963, when I was finally making enough money so Barbara could get off the road and return to Maryland. And believe me, by this time she was ready to go home.

The only problem was, we didn't really have one. A home, that is. That's when I started thinking about how it might be time to put down some roots, a place we could always return to that was ours and ours alone.

We looked for quite a while to find something we could afford, out in the country with a little acreage. It was Barbara's brother, Donny, who actually found the perfect place for us, in Davidsonville, Maryland, that became our first real home.

In 1961, I recorded my first four instrumentals for Capitol Records. Two of them, "Under the Double Eagle" and "Black Sapphire," surprised everyone at the label, but no one more than me, by getting a lot of airplay. Instrumentals, it seemed, made for good programming, because disk jockeys could read a commercial over them before going to a ballad—by someone else.

Still, the radio exposure, such as it was, led to the recording of my all-instrumental first album, *The Lightning Fingers of Roy Clark.* Ken Nelson, who produced the album, wrote some very funny liner notes for the back: "As in the days of the old west, when the fast gunfighters would come to town and all the young gunfighters would try to challenge him to see if they were as fast as he was, here comes a young, fast guitar player that all the others are now setting their sights on to see if they can play as fast as *The Lightning Fingers of Roy Clark.*"

While I was making the album, I also recorded two "black" songs: a Ruth Brown hit, "As Long as I'm Moving," and one called, "Talk about a Party." Because no one knew who Roy Clark was, both songs started getting airplay, *mostly on all-black radio stations!*

At a record convention in Chicago, a contingent of black radio representatives went to the Capitol Records booth to congratulate the label for having signed a new black performer. Capitol then considered rushing out a Roy Clark album without showing my face. For the cover, they wanted to put a picture of a musician in silhouette! I think what they envisioned was an album entitled, "The musical melodies of Leroy Clark!" They probably would have done just that if I hadn't started getting some national television exposure and people began to see what I looked like, and learned that I definitely wasn't black!

That all came about in 1962, when Jack Paar, who had become a national sensation as the host of "The Tonight Show," decided to step down from what had been one of the most powerful and influential shows in television, and NBC signed Johnny Carson to replace him. Because Carson had six weeks left on his contract at ABC as the host of the popular game show "Who Do You Trust?" and NBC wanted to create a sort of buffer zone between Paar's regime and Johnny's, the network decided to use a series of guest hosts for the interim period of time.

One of those guest hosts happened to be my old boss, Jimmy Dean, whom I had seen and heard very little from since he'd fired me. I wasn't really surprised by his success. I knew if anyone was ever going to make it to the big time, it would be Jimmy. It was something he had focused his entire life on achieving. What did surprise me was when I was working a club in Safford, Arizona, in the Hotel Buenavista, and got a call from him out of the absolute blue. He was furious, because he hadn't been able to track down either Jim Halsey or me. "What does your manager have," he screamed into the phone, "an unlisted number?"

In typical Jimmy Dean fashion, he found me by calling every club he thought I might possibly be playing. He had started on Monday morning and finally found me on Wednesday night. He said he had been trying to get hold of me because he was hosting "The Tonight Show" and wanted me as a guest for that Friday night.

I felt just great about this, especially after all that had gone down between us. I asked the club owner if he would let me out of my weekend commitment, and he said of course. So, after the Thursday show, I got into my car and drove from Safford to Tucson, where I caught a late-night flight to Phoenix. From there I boarded a plane to Chicago, changed for one bound for New York, where I finally arrived at one o'clock Friday afternoon.

I took a taxi right to the studio, and without taking so much as an extra breath rehearsed two numbers with the band, an instrumental tune, and "The Great Pretender." The producers suggested I might want to have a third song ready as a possible duet with Jimmy. He was off rehearsing in another part of the building; I still hadn't seen him until just before we went on the air, and had no idea whether or not we would, in fact, perform together.

When I finally did see him backstage, it was quite a reunion. We threw our arms around each other, hugged and reminisced about the old D.C. days. Then Jimmy asked me how many tunes I was doing.

I said, "Two, possibly a third, with you."

He said, "You'll do the two, and if that don't get 'em, you'll do two more. When you leave here tonight you're going to be tall hog at the trough."

My album had been out for about four months when I did my numbers on "The Tonight Show," and it was selling pretty well. However, after my appearance that Friday night, thanks to the power of television, it took off and became a best seller.

Suddenly, Capitol Records sat up and for the first time noticed that I was actually on their label! I then discovered they had publicity and promotion branches all over the country. I found out because each branch was sent a package marked "URGENT." Inside was a memo attached to the album that read, "Because of the recent appearance of Roy Clark, our artist, on the Tonight Show, there has been renewed interest in this album."

As for the engagement in Safford, I had played there a week and a half prior to my television appearance, and did good business. After "The Tonight Show" that Friday night, I jumped back on a plane, arrived in Safford just in time for Saturday's shows, and found I couldn't even get into town without a passport! I mean, they were standing ten deep around the walls of the club. The entire hotel was packed, the lobby filled with people waiting to get in, people spilling out onto the street. I had been traveling for two days, I was tired, and for the first few seconds after I arrived at the club, I wondered who it was they had booked while I was gone. I had no idea what was going on.

I mean, it was sheer pandemonium! Out of appreciation to the owner, I did three complete shows that night for three completely different audiences packed so tight no one could move! Even so, the club was able to hold only about two hundred people, so hundreds wound up being turned away. They had come from as far away as Phoenix, Tucson, and New Mexico, just to see me!

Joe Allison, who at the time was an independent producer and songwriter—remember "He'll Have to Go"?—was also a top disk jockey on KFOX in Long Beach, California, and on the Armed Forces Network. Joe had first heard of me when Hank Penny's wife, Sue Thompson, brought him in to see me perform at the Golden Nugget. Sue was a successful singer with several hit records, including "Norman," "Sad Movies (Make Me Cry)," and "James (Hold the Ladder Steady)."

Joe had a working relationship with Ken Nelson, and after my "Tonight Show" appearance, told Ken he should let me sing on record. Joe said he thought I "read" a great song. I believe he compared me to Frank Sinatra—not my voice, but the way Sinatra not only sings a song but "tells" it as well. His phrasing is about the best there is.

Anyway, Joe got permission from Ken for me to do a cover version of the "B" side of a Bill Anderson record, "The Tips of My Fingers." When Joe first played it I thought it was a great song, one that I could really do something with. He then found an arranger, Hank Levine, who orchestrated it for thirty musicians.

The recording session was scheduled to take place at the Capitol Tower's studio B, in Hollywood. Joe and I arrived early and met with Hank Levine about forty minutes before the actual session time. We were soon joined by Ken Nelson, whose offices were on one of the top floors of the tower. As we were standing around talking, all these musicians started coming in. Viola players, violinists, horns, an upright bassist, a cellist, a pianist, and six voices! Ken kept watching the studio fill up. Finally he said, "I thought you boys were using studio B today."

Joe said, "We are."

"Ah, then," Ken said, "these musicians must all be in the wrong studio."

Joe laughed and said, "No, they're with us."

Ken blanched! From a casual go-ahead to cut a vocal, which he figured might need maybe five country pickers, tops, he was suddenly surrounded by thirty musicians! Well, he just about lost it. There was no way he could go to the brass and justify spending thousands of dollars on a Roy Clark session. He turned to Joe and said calmly, "You know this will cost me my career."

In those days, it took an enormous amount of time to record a full orchestra, which, in effect, was what we had. Everything had to be balanced, with instruments and vocals recorded more or less "live," captured perfectly on a complete take. It seemed like forever before we finally were ready to do a first run-through. Ken, meanwhile, was in the booth, breaking the points off dozens of pencils, pulling his hair out, wondering where he was going to look for a new job.

When we finally finished, we had a record that began with strings, all the way from the bottom of the scale to the top, followed by my vocal:

> *I had you,*
> *Right on,*
> *The tips of, my fingers . . .*

Afterward, Ken walked up to me, put his arm around my shoulder and said, "Well, I was really worried, but not anymore. I believe we have a big hit on our hands."

He was right.

"The Tips of My Fingers" was released in the spring of 1962 and really took off. It was not only a huge country hit but a legitimate crossover success as well. It stayed on the pop charts for twenty-six weeks, where I believe it peaked at number six.

To help promote it, I played big record hops and did numerous local TV shows throughout America and Canada.

I played a spring rock hop down in Birmingham, Alabama, in this big coliseum, packed to the rafters with fifteen- and sixteen-year-old screaming kids. There I was on the same bill with all these teenage rock groups!

It was the first time I'd seen amplifiers stacked on top of each other, from the floor of the stage to the ceiling. Everything was so loud the only way you could tell when one act went on and came off was just that the roar from the audience got louder. I turned to the guy who had hired me and said, "Can I ask you something? Why am I here with all these groups who are going, *oo, ba, ba, ba, ba, ba, ba, ba, bada ba dah,* which I have to follow with 'I reached out my arms...'"

He said, "Because I love your record and I thought it would give a nice balance to the show." I thought for certain I was going to get booed off the stage, but, hey, the kids were great to me. I was amazed.

I even made an appearance on Dick Clark's "American Bandstand," which seemed truly amazing to me. Here I was, thirty years old, playing to a studio audience of kids treating me like a rock star!

The song was so successful, first chance I had, Ken Nelson brought me back into the studio to record an album called *The Tips of My Fingers,* which also did very well. Because my recording career, which was now becoming firmly established, every other phase of my professional life got a piggyback boost.

I started playing bigger venues, billed as the star on the same package tours I had once been the extra added-on performer. I was becoming so popular no one wanted to follow me! All the other acts suddenly had to catch the same early flight. In a strange way, this really hurt my feelings, because I was working with some of my idols, people I highly respected, who, it seemed, suddenly didn't want to have anything to do with me. When Hank Snow didn't want to follow me, I became a little confused. It wasn't a heavy emotional thing, it didn't leave lasting scars, but at the time I didn't understand it. All my life, whenever and wherever I was booked, my attitude was, *look out, Hoss, here I come, throw it up and see if it sticks to the ceiling,* and I thought everyone else was the same way.

By 1965 I had developed something of a name and had a little money in the bank, which meant that now when I toured, I could stay in better hotels and eat better food, without going down the price list before making my choices.

I continued playing dates and making records, and as I did so my career began to take a subtle but significant change in direction. I was becoming as well known for my appearances on television as I was for my records and concerts ever since I had made my first appearance on "The Tonight Show" with Johnny Carson in 1963.

I discovered I had a natural rapport that made it seem as if Johnny and I had been buddies forever. Johnny not only felt comfortable around me, he was the first guy who ever got me to really just talk on television, rather than doing *schtick* or telling jokes. In the past, on every television show I was ever on, when in doubt, I always fell back on a funny face, or a clever line. When I watched the show that night on TV, I realized just how brilliant Johnny Carson was at what he did. After that first appearance, I was told by the producers that I had an open invitation, any time I wanted to be on the show.

"The Tonight Show" opened up a lot of doors for me. I began to appear regularly on a lot of TV talk shows. Then, in 1966, I heard again from my old friend Jimmy Dean. He was a big star now, with his own weekly prime-time television variety program on the ABC network, and he wanted me on as a guest.

I went up to New York to do his show. All the variety shows came from either Los Angeles or New York in those days. I arrived on a Sunday night for a week of rehearsals, and did the show the following Friday night.

The next night, I was booked to play a college homecoming in Ada, Oklahoma, where I was scheduled to open for Mel Tormé. The homecoming was a big social event for the city. We were appearing in a good-sized auditorium packed so tight it was hard to breathe. The emcee came out and said, "And now, a young man that you saw last night on . . . ," and that's as far as he got before the place erupted. Over the cheers, he finished his introduction, ". . . on the Jimmy Dean show . . . that guitar wizard . . . Roy Clark!"

Jimmy Dean may not have been all that hot in New York City but he was a very big deal in Oklahoma. Everybody there that night had seen me on TV the night before. I mean, there was magic in the air! I was it, and could do no wrong. I walked out and tripped and they gave me a standing ovation! I mean I destroyed them! The parting of the Red Sea couldn't have followed my act! They were still screaming and throwing babies in the air for fifteen minutes after I left the stage!

Meanwhile, Mel Tormé, who didn't know me from Adam, was watching from the wings, and started worrying. When it was his turn he went out on stage and did everything he could think of, things he hadn't done since he was a child. I mean he tap-danced, he did back-flips, he played drums, piano, he screamed, he hollered, he even sang! However, no matter what he did, the audience's reaction was, that's all right pal, but where's the guy with the guitar? It was just my night.

John Hitt, an agent who worked with Jim Halsey and later became my manager, had booked the show, and driven up with Mel from Oklahoma City in his, John's, big Lincoln. After the show, John dropped me off at the bus station, where I waited in the drizzling rain to catch my bus back to Oklahoma City. I was standing there with my guitar and a little cardboard suitcase with a rope around it, a pitiful look on my face, as the Lincoln took off down the road. John later told me they drove for twenty-five miles before Mel, who up to this point hadn't said a word, turned and said, "Don't you ever, ever, *EVER* book me with that hillbilly son-of-a-bitch again!!"

Tall hog at the trough...

Yesterday, When I Was Young

5

As I continued to do television, my reputation grew as a TV entertainer who sang country music, as opposed to a country music
artist who appeared on TV.

Which was all well and good, except that because of it I
wasn't getting all that much support from my record label.
Since Capitol was such a mainstream "pop" oriented company,
it was difficult for any country singer under the best of circumstances to get much attention from them. When "The Tips
of My Fingers" really began to make some noise, Jim Halsey
begged Capitol to take out some ads for it in the trades. They
absolutely refused until Halsey actually shamed them into it.
He said if they would pay a third of the cost of the ads, the
publisher would pay a third and so would we.

As you might have imagined, I was no longer enamored
with Capitol Records. What finally made me ask to be let out of
my contract was an incident that happened early in 1967. I had
become pretty much of a regular on "The Tonight Show," and
whenever I had a new record about to be released, the producers wanted me to come on and introduce it. What per-

former could ask for a better deal than that? And what label wouldn't kill for that kind of exposure? The answer to the first question is no one. The answer to the second? I'll let you fill it in. Here's a clue.

As it happened, early that year I did have a new record coming out. I called the show, and they said sure, great, come on down! I gave them the release date, they booked me, and then at the last minute, Capitol bumped the record's release back four weeks. "The Tonight Show" said no problem, just call with the new release date. I did just that, then had to cancel my appearance again when Capitol chose, without any explanation, to delay the release of the single another six weeks.

This happened with every Capitol release I had, and although "The Tonight Show" never seemed to have a problem with it, I sure did. Finally, Halsey and I sat down and talked things over, after which, at my insistence, he called Ken Nelson and told him I wanted off the label.

Ken told Jim, "I can't believe it! I can't believe Roy wants to leave Capitol Records! This has got to be managerial talk. You want a better deal and you want more money, right? Roy doesn't really want off. If Roy wants off you have him call me himself."

Well, hey, I thought that was one of the reasons I had a manager. It's hard for me to make those kinds of calls, but this time I knew I had to. I called Ken and told him I wanted out. He asked me to come up to see him, which I did.

Now, every time I went up to the Capitol Tower, I felt like I should put on a name tag that said, "Hi. My name is Roy Clark and I record for your company," because nobody "upstairs" knew who I was. Not a one of them. When I arrived at Ken's office, he had all these computer printouts thick as phone books on his desk. After exchanging pleasantries, he said to me, "Roy, the reason I can't demand a firm release date for your records is, well, look at the last album you recorded, 11073."

Everything in record companies is numbers, not titles. "Oh," I said. "You mean *The Tips of My Fingers* album."

"Whatever, it came out and didn't sell ... hunh ... I didn't realize it sold that well ... a hundred fifty thousand copies ... that's good, that's real good. But let's look at this one ... "

He read off another number. "You mean *The Incredible Roy Clark* album?"

"That's the one ... it only did ... wait a minute. I'll be darned, I didn't know it sold that well ... a hundred and forty thousand albums ... well, let's go on ... "

He had to search hard for one that sold only seventy-five thousand! It always surprised me and in a funny way made me feel good that my own producer didn't know how well my albums had done. In fact, I was selling an average of a hundred thousand albums with every release. In country music back then, that was pretty doggone good, especially since Capitol did hardly any promotion for me on its own. They just put my records out there, and if they sold, fine.

At the end of that meeting, Ken realized I meant what I had said. He sat back, put his palms up, and told me, "Roy, if you're not happy here, it's not going to work. I think you're making a big mistake, but if you want off the label, I won't stop you."

With that, my seven-year association with Capitol Records came to an end.

I immediately received a lot of offers from other labels, but none were willing to give me the kind of release guarantee and promotional commitment I wanted. I finally told Halsey I'd rather not record at all than go through the same mistreatment again.

So I stayed out of the studio until a record company came along that better understood what the business was supposed to be about. Dot Records was an aggressive little independent company that seemed to me to be more "with it" than the so-called majors. It was owned by a fellow named Randy Wood, who began it in Gallatin, Tennessee, a suburb of Nashville, as essentially a mail-order operation. As the label grew, Randy eventually relocated his operation to California, signed up larger acts, most notably Pat Boone, and Dot began to be recognized as a label to contend with.

When they first approached Halsey and me, we liked the direction they appeared to be taking, and, something even more important, we liked Randy's attitude. He said he would be honored to have me on his label, and hey, let's make some records together! That sounded like a really good idea to me, so I told Halsey, yeah, let's sign on.

A lot of the greatest things that happen in the music business come about more often as the result of some happy accident than any planned event. In fact, one of my biggest hits happened just that way. I was in Nashville to record an album for Dot Records. I was sitting in my hotel room one night after a session when Joe Allison, my record producer, and Scotty Turner, who was then a record producer and songwriter with Liberty Records, dropped by with a new song they said I should consider recording. As it happened I was just about finished with the album, and was scheduled to leave town for a couple of days before returning for one final session, so I wasn't that eager to learn any new material.

Scotty said, "This is a great song that doesn't fit any of the artists I'm currently recording. I really think you could do it, Roy. You could really sing this song." Joe agreed, so I said, okay, let's hear it. Scotty ran up to his room and got the tape. I had a little reel-to-reel tape recorder in my room, and when he returned, Scotty put on this demo, a guy playing the piano and singing.

Well, what can I say? I was blown so completely away I literally fell out of my chair! Every line of that song was about my life. There wasn't a single word that didn't make total sense to me. "Yesterday, When I Was Young" is, in my opinion, the ultimate song.

It was originally written in French by Charles Aznavour and had already been a big hit in Europe for something like five years. The reason no one had covered it in English was that Aznavour did not approve of any of the English translations. There's something about the French language, I think, that allows men to say things in very expressive ways, without feeling embarrassed, the way the English and Americans some-time are. A lot of lyricists had tried and failed to translate the song without losing its true meaning, until finally Burt Kertz-ner came up with a version Aznavour liked and approved.

I finished the album I was working on and took the tape of the song back home to Maryland. One night about a week later I went into Owen Bradley's recording studio in Mt. Juliet, Tennessee, had the lights turned down low and recorded it.

Dot, which had recently merged with ABC and become ABC–Dot, released it immediately. All the radio stations jumped on it, it became a "pick-hit" on many of them, and shot up on all the charts. I had never had a record do that before. My songs usually built slowly, moved up a little, stayed there, then maybe climbed a little higher.

"Yesterday, When I Was Young" became the biggest single I had to date, and its effect on my career was enormous. Besides being yet another huge crossover hit, it added a new dimension to my audience. When I first heard it I thought it was purely a man's song. Then I was reminded that men weren't the only ones who could feel this way. I also thought it was an older person's song, until lots of kids, eleven and twelve years old, started telling me that "Yesterday" was their favorite song, too. That's the kind of magic "Yesterday, When I Was Young" had.

My recording of "Yesterday, When I Was Young" opened a lot of people's eyes not only to what I could do but to the whole fertile and still largely untapped field of country music, from the Glenn Campbells and the Kenny Rogerses, right on through to the Garth Brookses and Vince Gills. I wasn't, by any means, the first to make the bridge, to appeal to the broader, more popular market. You'd have to go back to Hank Williams and Eddy Arnold, and even Tex Ritter and Roy Rogers to find out who was the first. But I like to think I had some hand in it on the strength of my recording of "Yesterday, When I Was Young."

The song was so good, Frank Sinatra's people wanted him to cover it. He listened to it, agreed it was a great song, but declined to record it after seeing how high my version had gotten on the charts. He said he couldn't afford to have a second recording of a Roy Clark record. Coming from Frank Sinatra, that was really a great compliment.

However, the ultimate one came from Charles Aznavour,

who, on his own, once the record became a hit, published the following open letter in all the trade magazines:

> Dear Roy:
>
> I was profoundly moved by your magnificent recording of "Yesterday, When I Was Young."
> It is a source of deep satisfaction to a composer when his song is interpreted with all the feeling and heart he intended.
> I wish to also convey my thanks to your creative producer, Joe Allison.
> Both of you have my sincerest congratulations and gratitude.
>
> Merci,
> Charles Aznavour

After "Yesterday," several more songs I recorded did very well. In fact, many developed followings all their own.

In 1971, I met with legendary songwriter Boudleaux Bryant, in Nashville. "Roy," he told me, "I wrote a song for you last night." Right then and there, he picked up a guitar and sang it:

> *Come live with me*
> *And be my love*
> *And share my bread and wine*
> *Be life to me, be wife to me*
> *Be mine*

I thought to myself, what a great song! I recorded it immediately and it not only became my first number one record but also the first number one for the House of Bryant publishing company. I had had some hits that had reached number two, number three, and number six, but that was my first number one, not only on the country charts, but the pop charts as well. Like "Tips of My Fingers" and "Yesterday," "Come Live with Me" proved to have strong crossover appeal.

By now, I was crossing over with just about everything I released, which, in a strange kind of way, didn't make me all that happy. At the time, a lot of country stations were only playing what they called "pure" country, and because of my crossover, they thought I was a little too pop. I would rather have been considered strictly a country singer, even though this was a time when a pure country record didn't seem to matter to anyone all that much. Practically speaking, you still had to cross over to make it with a national audience. It's funny, today everybody in pop seems to want to cross over to country. I guess it's all part of the unpredictability of this crazy business they call music.

For a while I recorded a lot of songs with "messages" in their lyrics, as opposed to straight-ahead love songs. "I Never Picked Cotton," was one. It sold pretty well, and to this day I still get requests to do it. "Right or Left at Oak Street" was another one. It had moderate sales, but a lot of people identified with it, as they did with "I Give You Music."

I continued to expand my professional realm, doing concerts in noncountry places, and more and more New York City–based television talk shows. I did shows with legitimate Broadway actors and actresses, who all seemed to know who I was. They'd say, "Hi Roy, how you doing? I love your recording of 'Yesterday' . . ."

I can't tell you how many people would come up to me after a show in Las Vegas, Reno, or Tahoe and say, now, I'm not a country music fan, I don't particularly like country music, but

I like you. I'd say, thank you very much, and think, boy, I'm about as country as it gets. I knew what they were really trying to say, that it was my *presentation* of country that made my music acceptable to them. They obviously weren't aware of all the really beautiful voices in country music, like Eddy Arnold and Jim Reeves, and the great jazz-influenced musicians like Bob Wills and Lefty Frizzell who made some of the finest music anywhere.

To me, "pure country" is defined by the music of Roy Acuff and the comedy of Minnie Pearl, both of whom, in my opinion, could cross over to any audience. I took Minnie Pearl with me to Las Vegas to open one time. I had loved her work for years, but just before we opened, I suddenly thought to myself, wait a minute, this is Las Vegas, these are hip audiences, what if . . . well, she destroyed them with the same old jokes she'd been telling for thirty years. I learned a good lesson that night. Humor is humor, talent is talent, and audiences are smarter than a whole lot of us sometimes give them credit for being.

Not long after the ABC–Dot merger, the label was bought out by Paramount, and became ABC–Paramount. Then MCA bought out ABC–Paramount, and the label's name was changed again, this time to MCA. Although I was wary about being attached to such a mainstream mega-label, I hoped for the best. Perhaps because I had demonstrated my ability to sell records, they would treat me differently than I had been treated by Capitol. And, for a while, things seemed all right. I had a fair measure of success at MCA and then they started playing with me. Let me explain.

I had always had the right of refusal for everything connected to the release of my music, including the design of the album covers. Although I was never totally satisfied with the packaging of my records, I always forgave the record companies. Maybe I wasn't available, maybe they couldn't reach me on the road, or I was overseas and they had to go ahead and make a decision. So I didn't really enforce that right of approval, until I did an album called *Roy Clark Sings Country Classics.*

When I finished recording it, I went in and posed for the album jacket photo. When the record came out, I got a copy of it and there I was on the cover, with a rose superimposed in my mouth! There wasn't a single rose song in the album, no hint at all anywhere of a rose, so, I wondered, why did I have one in my mouth?

I was angry. I hadn't approved this. But I figured it was too late to do anything about it now. The record was out, so I had to let it go. However, I made it clear to the executives at MCA that from now on, before they released any records of mine, I wanted to see the cover art first. Fine, they said.

Well, when the next album came out, they jacked with that one, too. I hadn't had time to sit for a regular photo session for the cover, so MCA suggested using a shot of a real nice country scene with meadows and trees. They showed it to me and I approved the cover. However, when they ran it through the printing process, the colors came out psychedelic, badly distorting what was supposed to have been a relaxed, pastoral scene. I called them up and said, "Now boys, I told you before how I feel, and I'm serious about it. You know I don't like to complain much about anything, but this is getting out of hand." They apologized and promised it wouldn't happen again.

The next album had a very special meaning for me. It was to be my first all-gospel recording. As a Christian with a very strong sense of faith, I have always felt guided by a force and a love, and protected, and because of that probably spared from a lot of things so maybe I could do some good in this world. Somehow, I felt this album might be one of those good things. It was, in my opinion, one of my better efforts. Larry Butler did a great job producing a smart set of contemporary gospel songs with good driving arrangements that really cooked. I was very proud of it, and determined to make sure it was packaged with the same care that went into the recording.

I was in Tulsa when MCA sent the artwork to me. We had debated for quite a while what to put on the cover. I suggested a little country church maybe, with me standing in front looking up at the steeple and the cross. No, they said, there've been a lot of those done lately. As my album had a contemporary sound, they thought a different kind of outdoor scene might work better.

We went down to Nashville and found an old cemetery with a lot of beautiful trees that everybody seemed to like. I posed for a photo in front of an old magnolia. Prior to the cover being finalized, Halsey made a point of calling MCA, to remind them how much the "rose" cover had upset me, and that I was going to exercise my right of approval for the cover of the gospel album. They said fine, no problem.

When the layout was finished, they sent it to me, and I thought it was actually pretty good, right down to the border that framed the photo. Okay, I said, I can live with this. MCA then sent the layout on to California, where the album's packaging was being done. I reminded them that after that, I wanted to see it again. Of course, they said.

I then went back on the road, and a couple of months later,

while I was playing the Music Fair in Boston, one of my people came backstage and said, "There's a little old lady out here who'd like you to sign your new album." I said, fine, bring her back. She handed me the album, and I was shocked to see it was my gospel record!

Not only had MCA not sent it back to me for final approval, *they had changed the cover!* Now the borders on the side of the picture were three times as wide, my face was blown up real big, and it looked as if I had a magnolia blossom growing out of my ear!

That's when the fit finally hit the shan! I called MCA and told them I was through, I'd had it, I didn't want to be on the label anymore. The executives at MCA seemed surprised by my reaction. I tried to explain to them how I felt, that it was like taking my baby and cutting her feet off! I stood my ground, and even though twenty thousand copies had already been sold, I enforced my contractual right of approval and insisted they recall the album. Obviously they couldn't get back the ones they'd sold. I think they retrieved about five thousand copies. I felt bad, because the album had taken off, and looked as if it might go on to be the biggest, most commercially successful record of my career.

MCA wound up eating the records they'd already pressed, and gave me my release. To this day, MCA still has the record. I've asked them for the masters, but haven't gotten them back just yet. I believe the album is just as relevant and timely today as it was when we made it, and I still hope someday to be able to release it.

MCA was my last major label. Once I was completely free, Halsey and I decided to start our own label, Churchill Records. We signed on a lot of the acts Halsey represented that, like me, were no longer on majors, singers like Hank Thompson, Rodney Lay, Ronnie Dunn, and Cindy Hurt. Although we produced what I believe was some of the finest country music being recorded anywhere, unfortunately, we just didn't have the distribution or financial backing to make a real go of it.

At this point, just as my recording career seemed about to go on the decline, my television career took an unexpected turn. In the summer of 1969, I had the opportunity to become part of a little one-hour network comedy special. I have to admit I wasn't very impressed with the concept. My initial reaction was that it couldn't do too much damage to my career. After all, I figured, no one would ever remember anything about a show the producers wanted to call "Hee Haw."

"Hee Haw"?

The Icing on My Professional Cake

6

I've often said that I didn't skip a single rung as I went up the ladder of success. There was never one career-defining moment that moved me overnight from being a nobody to being a somebody. Consequently, I put no more importance in playing the Frontier Hotel in Las Vegas than I did playing the Famous in Washington, D.C. The same thing goes for television. Playing live on local TV was just as important to me as any other shows I played. Each show was one more rung up that big ladder.

I was making a guest appearance on "The Jonathan Winters Show" in the fall of 1968 when I first met Frank Peppiatt and John Aylesworth, the producers, and Sam Lovullo, Jonathan's associate producer. All three would eventually form the nucleus for "Hee Haw," what I've always referred to as the icing on my professional cake.

By now, just about every variety show that came on the air wanted to book me as a guest. I was always open-ended about my appearances, one of the reasons I was invited back so many times. Instead of saying, hey, I've got a hit record I have to perform, I would always ask who else was on the show. If they said someone like Vic Damone, I'd say, okay, you have a male singer, I'll do an instrumental guitar tune.

I loved being on all the shows, each was a gas in its own way. However, when I was invited to appear on Jonathan Winters's program, it meant something special to me. He had always been one of my personal idols. Funny enough, when I first started appearing on television, a lot of people thought I was Jonathan Winters. There's a strong physical resemblance between us, particularly in our smile and the way we both are always rolling our eyes. So strong was the resemblance that a lot of press used to refer to me as "the musical Jonathan Winters." Folks would come up to me in airports and say, "Mr. Winters can I have your autograph?" I would always say I wasn't him, mainly because I didn't know how to spell Jonathan, otherwise it would have been easier just to sign the autograph!

Minnie Pearl and I were both booked to appear as guests by Sam Lovullo. I didn't know it at the time, but Jonathan was having trouble getting ratings in the South, and Sam came up with the idea of using country music guests as a way to increase the viewership. He booked Buck Owens, Minnie Pearl, Roy Rogers and Dale Evans, George "Goober" Lindsay, and me. Funny enough, whenever a country act was on, Jonathan's ratings went through the roof.

I remember the first time I walked into the studio to do the Winters show. I'd never met Jonathan before, and there he was sitting in the audience with one of his assistants, while the crew did camera set-ups. Out of the blue he turned to me, pointed to the set and said, "You see that house? Me and the brother bring fried chicken up there to the old folks and sit on the front porch..." Instead of saying hello, welcome to the show, he did a complete fifteen-minute spontaneous, original, and altogether brilliant routine.

After four or five days of rehearsals, just before we were ready to tape the show, Jonathan's two producers, John Aylesworth and Frank Peppiatt, told me they had an idea for a new show and wanted to know if I'd be interested in hosting it. They hadn't come up with a name yet, but they described the format to me. What they had in mind, they said, was a show with a lot of fast-paced comedy and blackouts, not unlike "Laugh-In," which was a big hit at the time. However, their show would emphasize country humor and country music.

They wanted two cohosts, and I believe they had already approached Buck Owens, who had a solid track record in country music sales. To balance out the show, they wanted a country personality with high television visibility.

Was I interested? Of course I was. I had learned a long time ago in this business you say yes to everything, because most things never happen. I gave them Jim Halsey's phone number, and left it at that.

A couple of months later—I believe it was in October— Halsey called to tell me Peppiatt and Aylesworth were ready to go ahead with the show. I said, "What show?"

"The one they told you about," Jim said. "That country comedy thing. They want to call it 'Hee Haw.'"

" 'Hee Haw'?"

"Yes. What do you think of that name?"

"Well," I said, "it's not great, but it doesn't bother me." It didn't at first, until the more I got to thinking about it and realized what a terrible name for a show it really was. "Laugh-

In" was a takeoff on the word "Laughin'." "Hee Haw" was a takeoff of "Laugh-In," one step removed, and to me one step less funny.

Still, I didn't say anything, I didn't think it mattered, believing the show was someone's pipe dream. I went out on the road, did my thing, played a lot of local variety television shows, had a good old time, while Halsey continued to meet with the two producers.

Early in 1969, CBS scheduled "Hee Haw" as a one-hour special, to be shot in Nashville. This happened just as the Smothers Brothers were having their big falling out with the network. As heavy hitters, and the Smothers Brothers definitely were that, they "owned" the summer time slot their Sunday evening prime-time program ran in during the rest of the year. That meant that when they took their summer vacation, they had the right of either producing or approving a show to fill in for them.

However, once CBS and the Smothers Brothers had their falling out over the political content of their shows and the show was canceled, a very sudden and desirable programming vacancy became available for the coming summer. The network, finding itself in a peculiar bind, went to Aylesworth and Peppiatt and asked if they could do twelve "Hee Haws" instead of just one. No problem!

What made their decision possible was the fact that the show was taped in Nashville. What the producers may have given up in production values, they more than made up with the abundance of available legitimate country talent. As soon as they got the order for twelve shows, all they really had to do was pick up a phone and call the performers they wanted, who could be ready to go on in an hour.

When I found out we were going to do twelve shows instead of one, I immediately canceled whatever personal appearances I had on the books. Still, I thought, twelve shows and that would definitely be it. Already, the consensus of everyone in country music, from the Country Music Association (CMA) to every big star, was no way could the show succeed. Worse, they warned, "Hee-Haw" might set back the progress of country music twenty years. At the time, the CMA was trying to create an urban country-western image of intelligent, educated people who played America's real music.

By contrast, everyone on "Hee Haw" was dressed in bib overalls, and the humor was decidedly "hillbilly." We went on network television literally scratching our groins, saying, "Well, I ain't never seed anything happen like this here before. What you think 'bout that, Luther?" Jim Halsey and I talked about it and agreed that doing the twelve shows wouldn't seriously damage my career. People would see me, yes, but almost before the shows were over, they would forget them and forgive me.

We taped the show at WLAC, Channel 5, CBS's local affiliate in Nashville. The studio facilities there were very small by network standards, space normally used for making local commercials. "Hee Haw" was always shot in segments. For that first show, they'd put a set up, we'd tape on it, they'd strike that one and put up another, and so on. On each one we did what they called "Hee Haw" jokes, which I have to tell you I thought were pretty cornball, on the level of, "Why did the chicken cross the road?" We're talking *primitive* here! While I didn't feel it was my place to say anything, if they had asked me my opinion, I would have told them, Give me five minutes I'll come up with much better material.

But they didn't, and I didn't; I performed the jokes they had, and groaned to myself afterwards. We taped without an audience, which also threw me. If there had been people to play off of, I might have at least had the benefit of that going for me. However, the studio was too small for that. As a result, there weren't even groans coming back at me to react to.

Luckily, I've always felt comfortable on television, even without a live audience, I guess because when I look at a camera I don't see a piece of equipment. I see people and faces. I never feel like I'm talking to anyone but real people. So for me, the fact that the camera was right there actually helped tremendously. To tell you the truth, I enjoyed doing those first twelve shows; I loved to tell jokes, even corny ones, and the show featured a lot of terrific music.

When we had completed about half the segments for the twelve shows, the producers put one together and screened it for the cast. When I saw it for the first time, I finally "got it." Now I understood what they were going after. Suddenly all those bad jokes made perfect sense to me. The show was really "created" in the editing—*joke, bam, skit, bam, song, bam, skit, bam, cornfield, bam, song, bam, here's Jackie Phelps and Jimmy Riddle doing the Eefin and the Hamboning on the leg, and We'll be right back in a minute after this commercial break.*

In the beginning, many top country artists refused to do the show. The producers didn't even go after them, because they knew they'd be turned down. On the other hand, a lot of up-and-coming talent was desperate for national exposure. As a result, we never hurt for guests.

"Hee Haw" debuted Sunday night, June 15, 1969. We were actually still taping when the first shows aired. Once CBS dropped the Smothers Brothers, they were able to switch us from Sunday night to Saturday night to keep the tradition of the Grand Ole Opry. When you think of country music and the Opry, you think of Saturday night.

Well, in spite of being panned by every critic in the country, including those in Nashville who called "Hee Haw" the worst thing that had ever happened to television, to country music, and to America, the show was an immediate hit. Only the audiences, it seemed, liked us. We became the major TV smash of the summer, which left CBS with an unexpected stepchild. We were a hit show with no scheduled time slot. Like everyone else, the network had no idea we would be so successful and had made no contingency plan to include us in its fall prime-time schedule.

The best they could do was to make us first alternate on the list of replacement shows. So, we went off the air in September 1969, at the start of the new fall season, and returned that December, as the midseason replacement for "The Leslie Uggams Show," CBS's first casualty of the new TV year.

As I mentioned before and I'm sure most of you know, my cohost on "Hee Haw" was Buck Owens, a major talent and one of the few legitimate legends in the history of country music. I knew Buck for a long time before the show, going all the way back to an early Hap Peeples two-week tour through Canada on which we both were booked. We started in Vancouver and played our way across Canada, to Regina, Saskatchewan, and Alberta. We were supposed to go all the way to Montreal, until a bomb threat connected to the independence movement of the provinces at the time forced the local promoters to cancel the engagement. So the tour actually ended in Toronto. I came home and have never seen Montreal to this day.

Buck had one of the first commercially available Winnebagos, and the promoters for that tour arranged for me to travel with him. I'm sure Hap paid Buck a little extra to provide transportation for me. He was nice enough, but I remember thinking at the time that he was, shall I say, a little idiosyncratic in his behavior? He wasn't a laid-back country boy I felt comfortable being around. He was, and still is, very opinionated, very set in his ways, very dollar conscious. If he doesn't have the first dollar he ever made, he knows where it's at. What can I say, Buck is just a strange guy.

Now, Buck is very professional, and because he's so authentically country, makes certain demands in what some might consider an unsophisticated manner. I'm sure when Sinatra makes a demand, he does it with authority, whereas when someone like Buck wants something, he's liable to come off as petty.

I remember when we first started cohosting "Hee Haw," we were just learning how to get along with one another, and one night I came close to getting physical with old Buck. I knew if I let myself go it could get ugly, so I held back. Buck was on stage and got all over Sam Lovullo, an absolute sweetheart of a guy.

What happened was we were finishing up a taping, and Buck had plane reservations for a flight to California. He was about to leave when the producers discovered after checking the tape they were missing a camera shot. We were all forced to wait, and Buck kept on looking at his watch. Finally, like a real prima donna, he called Sam out of the control room and just got on him, "How dare you keep me waiting here!" he shouted, and in front of everybody got right in Sam's face. Now, Sam and I had by this time become good friends, and I thought for a moment about grabbing Buck by the throat and shaking his eyeballs together!

I've always believed that when you spend four or five days working on a television show, the production has to come first. Everyone has other plans, but you have to be flexible and able to make changes. Your primary responsibility has got to be to finish what you came to do.

I have to say, though, that I was a lot more experienced than Buck when it came to television, and eventually he learned how to make adjustments. For the great majority of the time, he and I proved a winning combination. I was thrilled to work with him and so many other talented people. It was a privilege to work with the likes of Stringbean, and my old friend Grandpa Jones. The Hagar Twins were a terrific duo. They'd been working for American Airlines vacuuming airplanes late at night before they were discovered by "Hee Haw." The girls, Lulu Roman, Jeannine Riley, and Gunilla Hutton from "Petticoat Junction," all joined us that first season, and were great fun to work with as well.

I also came to appreciate "Hee Haw's" ability to help expose the best of the up-and-coming country artists. Because the producers didn't really know who was big and who wasn't, they booked acts right out of *Billboard* magazine's country chart. That's why, for the first several years of the show, if you didn't have a song on the chart, you couldn't get on "Hee Haw," one of the things that helped make us a very hot show.

The Empty Arms Hotel in Cornfield County segment of "Hee Haw" served as a catch-all set for cast members to come in and do skits with me. I was the clerk. It was the natural place for all the guests to "check in." I also did a character called Claude Strawberry, the cornfield country poet. I straddled a thin line with that one. Claude was a sissy, you understand, but he wasn't gay. Still, I got a lot of letters from gay organizations wanting me to come out of the closet and support them. I said, boy, is something not getting through the way I want it to!

"Pickin' and grinnin' " was a segment that was just an excuse for the entire cast to get together. Dr. Campbell's office was the vehicle for Archie Campbell's brand of humor. Archie had been doing country comedy for years, and the producers felt the show needed an Archie Campbell to give us real country credibility.

And, of course, there was the one and only, irrepressible Junior Samples, out of Cumin, Georgia! Before "Hee Haw," Junior, who had a third grade education, worked in a sawmill, drove in stock car races, fished, and made moonshine whiskey. He had worked in a still from the age of nine, and had his very own by the time he was eleven.

Junior was authentic Americana. As such he really personified what "Hee Haw" was supposed to be all about, and added just the right lovable redneck buffoon image the show needed. If you asked someone familiar with the show, "What is a 'Hee Haw'?" he or she could show you a picture of Junior Samples and say, this is it.

Well, Junior, like I say, had a third grade education. He didn't know too much about anything "worldly," but you could talk to him about making moonshine whiskey, and he'd sound like a Harvard professor! Junior could make moonshine out of linoleum. The last time the Feds nailed him he had sixty-five thousand dollars' worth under a tarpaulin in the woods waiting for shipment. The judge finally told him, "Junior, this is it. No more slaps on the wrist and fines. The next time we catch you, it's prison." I believe that was what finally scared Junior out of the business.

Not long after, Junior's brother went down to the Gulf and caught a sea bass that weighed something like sixty pounds. He brought the head back to Georgia, and Junior put it in the back of his brother's pick-up and took it to a stock car race, and people marveled at it. Junior told them he caught it in a freshwater lake right there in Georgia. "My God," everyone said, "that has got to be the biggest fish ever caught in these parts!"

He then went on a local radio program to talk about the fish. The DJ asked him where he caught it. Junior said it came out of a local lake, and that he wasn't sure how much it weighed, but that there were seven in his family and they had eaten on it for a week. The phone lines lit up with people laughing their heads off.

Word soon filtered back to the state game commission. They sent investigators down from Atlanta. When they started questioning him, Junior got a little scared and confessed his brother had really caught it in the Gulf of Mexico. However, by this time a tape of the radio show had circulated around. Archie Campbell heard it, made a script out of it, went down to Georgia, found Junior, and took him into a recording studio. They made a record out of the fish story that became a country comedy best seller. When the producers started putting "Hee Haw" together, Archie suggested they get hold of Junior Samples. They brought him in, put him on camera, and as soon as they saw him realized he was exactly what they were after.

THE "HEE-HAW" YEARS

Buck and me on the set of "Hee-Haw."

Me and Junior Samples on "Hee-Haw" in 1975.

37

38

1975. Left to right: my father, Uncle Paul Clark, me,
Shot Jackson (behind me), Uncle Dudley Clark, Bob Shott,
Kenny Clark (behind Bob Shott), and Buck Trent.

The whole "Hee-Haw" gang.

Senator Robert Byrd fiddlin' around on "Hee-Haw."

40

Me, Billy Carter, and Grandpa Jones.

41

Here I am with my "look-alike," Jonathan Winters, in the "Hee-Haw" cornfield in the early 1980s.

42

43

Picking out a tune backstage at "Hee-Haw."

44

Buck and me with two of the "Hee-Haw" girls.

45

Barbara and me at the ranch in Mounds, Oklahoma, in 1978.

46

Behind the controls of a 1943 Stearman.

47

With the great Minnie Pearl in 1978.

On the "Merv Griffin Show" around 1979.

48

49

With Flip Wilson.

During one of my "Tonight Show" hosting stints. The guests that night were Suzanne Somers, Tammy Wynette, and George Jones.

GEORGE JONES   JIM STAFFORD   MEL TILLIS

MINNIE PEARL   ROY CLARK   TAMMY WYNETTE

GEORGE GOBEL   MARGO SMITH   GEORGE LINDSEY

An all-country "Hollywood Squares." Look who they put in the center.

With Barbara Mandrell.

Glen Campbell, Mel Tillis, Waylon Jennings, and me stopping for a picture during the taping of the soundtrack album for the film "Uphill All the Way."

With Engelbert Humperdinck.

Welcome TO THE OPRY FAMILY!
ROY CLARK
AUG. 87

It was a long time coming but I finally made it.

With three legendary performers, Minnie Pearl, forever in bloom, the late Dottie West, and my pal Jimmy Dean.

My dream come true. The Roy Clark Theater in Branson, Missouri.

On the links with Charlie Pride.

58

Backstage with the great Reba McEntire at the Bally Grand in Las Vegas.

59

60

With my long-time buddy Hank Thompson.

With my manager, Jim Halsey, celebrating 25 years together.

61

With John Hitt.

62

63

Barbara and me with the great Bob Hope.

My "miracle child," Davi Sallee.

64

65

A big welcome at the Roy Clark Elementary School in Oklahoma.

66

A room full of music, cars, and memories, with my dad.

67

A recent picture of Mom and Dad.

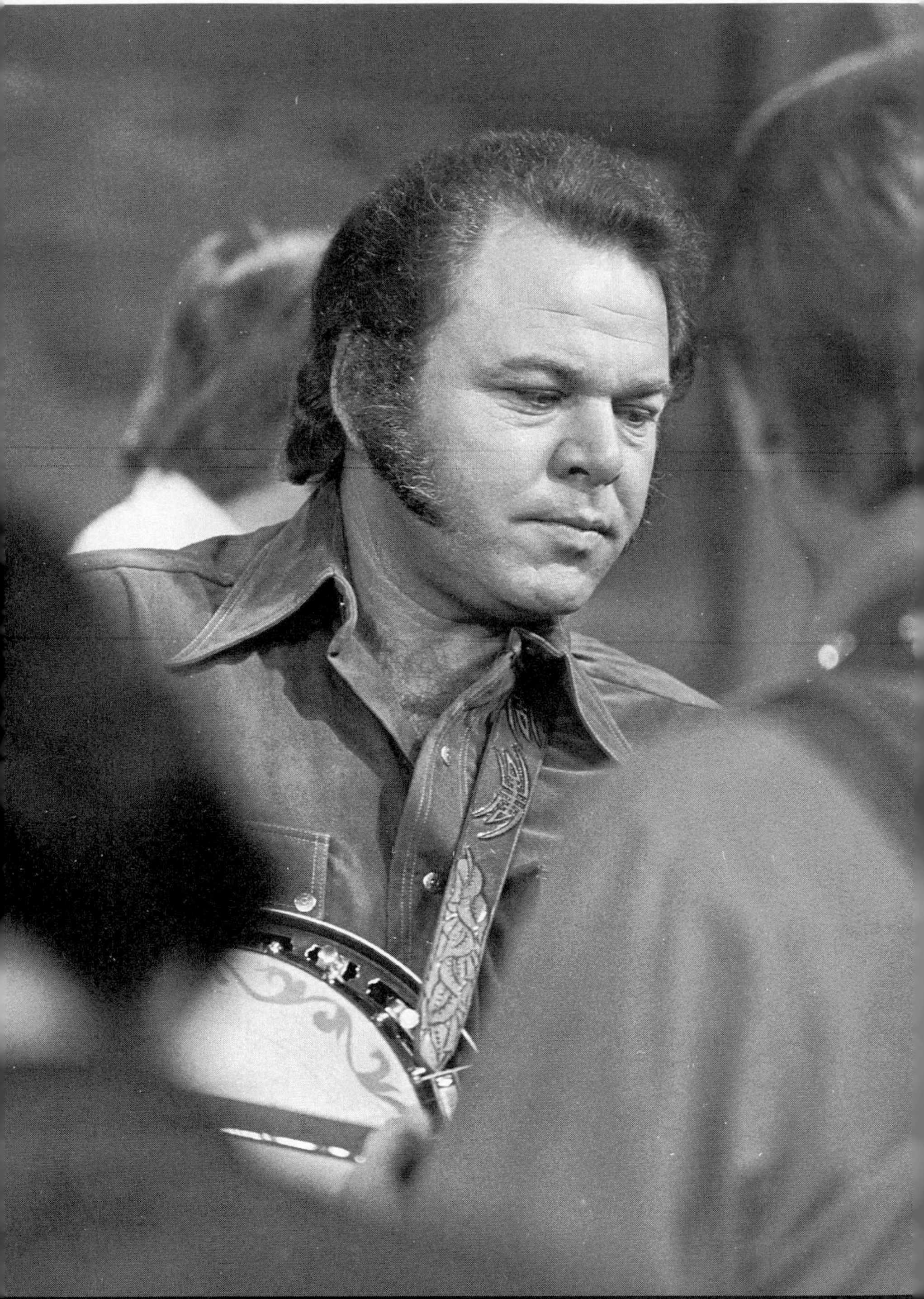

68

Now, one day, about a week after he joined the show, Junior turned to me and said he had seen me on a lot of other television shows. He didn't know who Buck was, he said, but he knew me. After a pause, he said, "Roy? Can I ask you something?"

"Sure, Junior."

"How did you get into this business?"

I went back and told him the whole saga, starting with how I used to play banjo with my dad. After a while, he looked over to me and said, "Huh! I just told a lie about a fish and here I am!"

As I mentioned earlier, the way the show worked, a scheduled day of taping had to be completed before anyone was allowed to leave, after which that set would be struck and a new one put up for the next day. That's why, if there was a problem, technical or otherwise, we had to keep going until we finished.

Well, during one of these long nights, I turned to Junior and said, "When this session is through, I'm going to need a drink of hard liquor." I was then called back to redo a bit, and later, in my dressing room, Junior found me and said, "Was you serious about that hard liquor?"

I said, "It was just something I said, I guess," and he replied, in a soft voice out of the side of his mouth, " 'Cause I got some out in the car. 'Course it's hot, and I ain't got nothin' to chase it with 'cept pork and beans . . . ."

I said, "Pork and beans to chase whiskey?"

"Oh yeah," he said. "It's good. It really works. One time I was in the car going somewhere and I wanted me a drink,

ROY CLARK

and I didn't have anything in the car. I reached under the seat and there was a can of pork and beans. So I popped the lid and took me a big old swig of that whiskey and a mouthful of those pork and beans and it kicked it just like that, really good!"

I told him as politely as I could that I didn't think I was ready for pork and beans and whiskey.

With Junior, what you saw was what you got. If "Hee Haw" was an attempt to go back a hundred years in American country culture, then Junior was the original prehistoric man. I've often said that he's the only one who came out of the country, went on TV, was introduced to the world, and actually regressed!

When we finished taping the initial twelve episodes, the producers threw a fancy party in a penthouse atop the Life and Mutual Insurance Building in Nashville. By now it was clear to everyone, including the network, that the show was going to be a hit, and we were all out to celebrate. Junior in particular was throwing it back pretty good.

The vice-president of CBS was there, along with a lot of other executives from New York. It was arranged that the cast would greet the network men as we walked through the door. They were all in black tie. A lot of us didn't have tuxedos, so we wore suits and ties.

Junior arrived, and he was just wasted. He walked in wearing his trademark bib overalls. When Junior got up in the morning he put on his tee-shirt, bib overalls, and ball cap, and was dressed for any function he ever had to attend in his life. I never saw him in anything else but that outfit. For this special occasion somebody gave him a tuxedo jacket and he put it on right over his overalls and tee-shirt.

Just inside the door there was a big buffet, and in the center of it a succulent, beautiful, forty-pound prime rib roast, pre-sliced and laid over. The first thing Junior did was reach over to the platter and grab a slab of it with his hands. He lifted it to his mouth, and as he did so the juice, oil, and grease just dripped right down to his elbow onto his clothes. As he gnawed on it like a dog, somebody from the show thought it was a good idea to get Junior through the greeting line as quickly as possible and then the heck out of there!

So they made him put down the prime rib, cleaned him up as best they could, and introduced him to the vice-president of CBS. One of the producers said, "Junior, this is the vice-president." And without batting an eye, he said, "Nice to meet you, Mr. Sparyou Agnew."

After Junior became famous, he thought he had to live up to his image in public and actually become "Junior Samples." For instance, he had a very nice set of teeth, but when he saw that a lot of country comics blacked out their front teeth, he went and had his pulled!

Eventually, some of the fame went to Junior's head. I happened to be standing beside him one time when a woman came up and asked him for his autograph. He said, "I don't have time now, I have to go eat."

She walked off and I said, "Junior, you was a little strong with that lady." Then I went ahead and signed some autographs. While I was doing that I heard him call her back and told her he'd be happy to sign that autograph. All I had to do was get his attention, and he was all right again.

He wasn't very old when he had a heart attack and passed on. He just didn't take care of himself. He drank a terrific amount, even though he had diabetes. He ate anything and everything, and because of it was extremely overweight. For all the things that were wrong with him he should have been under a doctor's care, but that wouldn't have made any difference to Junior. He's gone now, and I miss him. He was one of the key components to the success of "Hee Haw," and a truly great friend.

I believe we were on CBS for a total of two and half years when the network decided to cancel the show. We were forced out by Fred Silverman, who had come aboard as CBS's new program director. Every head of programming wants to leave his mark, and in order to do so, will try to shake things up. Silverman's big complaint when he took over was, in his words, "CBS's rural image." He didn't want to continue to be known as the head of the "barnyard network."

And, to a certain extent, CBS was just that. It had "Green Acres," "Beverly Hillbillies," "Petticoat Junction," "Andy Griffith," "Gomer Pyle," and "Hee Haw" on its prime-time schedule, every one of which was a winner in the ratings, by the way. However, it was not the image Silverman had in mind.

He obviously wasn't a fan of country music, and in that way he fit right in with the rest of the networks' so-called urban corporate mentality. To this day there is a segment of New York City–based television that has yet to accept country. Although for years "Hee Haw" made lots of money for CBS, I believe they still don't want very much to do with country music, or to be associated with what they think is its image.

Back then, they certainly didn't know what they had with us, or where the key lay to our appeal. For instance, we literally had to force the network to let us do gospel music on "Hee

Haw." Every country show since the history of time has included a segment of gospel music. Grandpa Jones fought for it and kept on being turned down by the network. Finally he came to me and said, "Roy, don't you think we ought to do some gospel?"

I said, "You're doggone right we should." I went to Sam Lovullo, who, when he saw that I was serious about it, went to bat for us and finally convinced the network, and of course the weekly gospel number became one of the most popular and enduring segments of the show.

We went on to sell hundreds of thousands of *Gospel Quartet* albums, recorded appearances of the material we did on the show. We had to whip the network suits to get them to let us release the albums, and when they became one of the hottest things ever to come out of the show, they said, to a man, hey, weren't we brilliant to think of *this* idea. Oh boy!

Before we were actually canceled, we were moved from eight o'clock Saturday night to eight o'clock Friday night. I guess Silverman figured viewers wouldn't be able to find us so fast, our ratings would drop off, and he'd have no problem shutting us down. Much to our relief, in spite of the move, we didn't suffer at all. As a matter of fact, our strong and loyal following probably had a lot to do with the phenomenal success of "All in the Family." That show, which debuted shortly after we did, immediately followed us in our original Saturday night time slot.

Then CBS moved us to Tuesday night, in a block of programming that included "Green Acres" and "Beverly Hillbillies" and gave the network a solid two hours of the dreaded "rural image." This proved a bit much for Silverman, and he wound up canceling all three shows just around the time ABC dropped Lawrence Welk. Although his ratings, like ours, were high, the boys upstairs at that network insisted he didn't attract the proper "demographics" either. In fact, a friend of mine and I made a little record about it, "The Lawrence Welk 'Hee Haw' Counter-revolutionary Polka." Like both shows, it, too, was a big hit.

After our cancellation, everybody involved with "Hee Haw" wanted to keep it alive. Although the producers had syndication offers, Sam Lovullo, who quit the network to become the producer of the show in syndication, Frank Peppiatt and John Aylseworth, who became its executive producers, and Nick Vanoff, the president of Yongestreet Productions, each owned a piece of "Hee Haw," and raised the money among themselves to form their own syndicate. Their intention was to keep the distribution rights for themselves, rather than leasing them to someone else. This was no easy task. I know that the creators of the show mortgaged their homes, and by doing so, jeopardized their futures as well, putting themselves into heavy debt to try to pull it off.

When they had the financing in place, they approached all the CBS affiliates that had carried the show when it was on the network, and gave them first option to continue carrying it. As I remember it, about ninety-nine percent of the stations signed up. In those areas where we hadn't been seen before, or were turned away by one affiliate, we were quickly picked up by another. In short order, instead of being on 165 network affiliate stations, we were now available on 228. As a result of being canceled, our viewing audience actually increased by a full third!

After that first December, when we replaced Leslie Uggams, there was never a single week when we weren't on television.

The only difference between being on the network and being syndicated was essentially financial. Instead of most of the money going to CBS, it went directly to the producers. Their gamble paid off and they became an extremely wealthy bunch of guys because of it.

This was their first time out of the chute, so there were some things they hadn't figured on. If you're a certain age, you'll remember when every kid in America carried a "Hee Haw" lunchbox and thermos bottle to school. There was a complete line of "Hee Haw" merchandise that, in its day, was as popular as Davy Crockett's coonskin hats had been in the fifties. Millions of dollars were made, most of it sheer profit, and none of it went to the show's producers. When CBS agreed to relinquish its rights to "Hee Haw," it did so as long as it could retain all merchandising. Apparently, even though the network didn't like the image of the show, they liked the money they could make off of it. It took years for the producers to renegotiate a deal for some of those rights. Was it worth all the hassle to do it? To tell you the truth, I would rather have had the merchandising rights than the profits from the show itself!

Through the years, with few exceptions, "Hee Haw" remained virtually the same from day one. Buck would open one show, I'd open the next, followed by the standard "Hee Haw" opening, then maybe a one- or two-liner, and the first commercial break. We'd come out of the commercial into music. Then it would be Buck's turn. The producers had a reel of Buck's tunes from which they could choose, and follow it with some comedy, maybe the barbershop, or the cornfield. If they did a moonshiner bit that called for a reaction from Junior, they could go to another reel filled with Junior "reaction shots."

I could tape everything I was involved with in two and a half to three weeks. Every June, the producers always taped more material than they actually needed. If we were scheduled to tape thirteen segments, we would actually wind up with enough material for fifteen or sixteen shows. Then, in October, we would reconvene and do the same thing. I've often said that "Hee Haw" doesn't have any outtakes. If someone blew a line, most times the producers opted to keep it in. The show was never overrehearsed, which, I think, is pretty obvious. I firmly believe that's one of the main reasons we lasted so long. I never saw a script ahead of time, as everything was on cue cards.

It became more like a family reunion than a work situation the two times each year we would all return to Nashville to tape the show. Everyone would arrive at the studio, see how fat everyone else had gotten, learn all the new babies' names, and go to it. We'd work from sunup to very late five days a week, until, just as everyone started to get a little tired and irritable, it would all be over until next time. I'd then go back on the road, do concerts, and forget about the show until it was time to tape some more material. Funnily enough, I rarely saw the show when it was broadcast, as I was always working Saturday nights, when it aired in syndication. That helped keep me fresh for the next set of tapings.

That's the way it went until 1991, when the producers decided they needed to make some changes. They wanted to cut out the cornfield, get rid of the animated donkey—the very symbol of "Hee Haw"—and eliminate the "pickin' and grinnin' " segment and moonshiners' still. In place of the cornfield they created a street scene, with a bus stop and a taxi pick-up, which they figured was more identifiable to younger folks who might not know what a cornfield was. The still was replaced by a neon stage, and a more contemporary, urban "mall" set was created for comedy skits.

With the sudden boom in country music, the media buyers—the advertisers—decided they needed to aim for a different demographic; namely, a younger audience. Hey, where had I heard that before? A lot of the older fellows were either no longer living or, like Buck, retired, and the decision was made to replace them with new "leading man" types. New girls were brought in as well, to replace the "old" ones. George Lindsay, Grandpa Jones, Gordie Tapp, Lulu, Linda Thompson, and I were the only original "Hee Haw" cast members held over.

A different opening theme was added, and the name of the program was changed to "The New Hee Haw Show." We "debuted" January 5, 1992. That night, some fifteen million "Hee-Haw" viewers tuned us in, sat back with their favorite beverage and found themselves watching a lot of fancy neon and strange new faces. They felt like they were watching a whole other show, and boy, did they let us know it.

The problem was, we had already taped and edited twenty-two shows that were in the can. Instead of taping in June and October, as we had always done in the past, the producers had decided to tape all twenty-two shows in October and November of 1991. The best way I can describe the reaction was that we had done the same thing Coca-Cola had when it tried to replace its "classic" soda with a new formula. It had that much of a negative reaction among our audience, which wanted the classic "Hee Haw" humor to remain intact.

In September of 1992, the producers wisely shelved the

new format and replaced it with "Hee Haw Silver," repeats of our best "classic" shows, none of which had been seen since they originally aired, with the exception of one rerun the same season they were broadcast. To many viewers, these shows, which were done more than twenty years earlier, were new shows. I went in and filmed a new bunch of wraparounds, with all the old cartoon-looking sets superimposed behind me, the cornfield, the moonshiners' still, the Empty Arms Hotel, the barbershop, and Doc Campbell's office.

There's also a silhouette of me superimposed with the donkey and the horseshoe, and the new "Hee Haw Silver" logo. I walk out, the camera pans down, the lights come up, and I say, "Hello, and welcome to another 'Hee Haw Silver.' Now the show you're about to see first aired in 1969, one of the first shows we did. On this show, you'll see that Grandpa Jones has a little trouble with his banjo and gets mad at it. This is also the first episode that featured Lulu's truck stop . . . So what do you say we watch the show together . . ."

We did fifty-two "Hee Haw Silver" shows, and were supposed to be leading up to a two-hour network special celebrating "Hee Haw's" silver anniversary. Nineteen ninety-three would have been our twenty-fifth broadcast season, making "Hee Haw," by the way, the longest syndicated television show in the history of the medium.

However, before that show could be produced, Sam Lovullo decided not to renew his contract. It was his feeling that "Hee Haw," in its original format, should have continued to be produced as such, so that, by tradition, we could have carried on with the look of the show that was most enjoyable, and that people wanted to see. He told management at that time that they should develop a different, more contemporary program that would utilize youth and country music and attract the big advertisers. He's now considering offers to create a new, contemporary country series for me.

Shortly before Sam left, the show had come under the control of a contingent of producers from Opryland Entertainment, who announced no new "Hee Haw" shows would be produced. I first found this out in March 1993, when I received a call from a reporter from the Associated Press, wanting to know my reaction!

Last fall, "Hee Haw" re-runs began airing Saturday nights on the Nashville Network, and quickly became TNN's highest rated program.

Through the years there was always talk about distributing the show in Europe, in all those television-starved countries. While we are heard in several countries over the Armed Forces Network, and shown on network television in Australia, the problem has always been that we would have to do some drastic editing, because foreign audiences would not understand basic hayseed comedy. They would certainly enjoy the music, and we could syndicate those segments overseas, but that would make us look more like a country video jukebox. In other words, a lot of "Hee," and very little "Haw."

The show changed my life in so many ways, not the least of which was how people reacted when they saw me in person. Before "Hee Haw," if I were flying commercially somewhere, I'd be on line to buy my ticket, people would see me and do a double take, with an "I think I know that guy," look on their faces. Occasionally they would ask if we knew each other and I'd say, "Well, I do television a lot." Some would then say, "You play the guitar, right?" Others would say, "Clark? Didn't I see you on television?" But after the show went on the air, it was, "Hey, Roy Clark, I see you every week on 'Hee Haw.'"

At the end of our first season I remember I had to fly to New York to do "The Tonight Show." I was living in Maryland, and Eastern Air Lines had a shuttle service that ran every half-hour from La Guardia to Washington National Airport. I used to do "The Tonight Show" in New York, catch a shuttle, and be home in time to watch it in bed when it aired that evening.

Well, this one time I arrived at the airport and boarded a plane, which was mostly dark except for the overhead reading lights. I had been one of the first passengers to board, and as I was sitting there, along came these three-piece Wall Street executive-types. One of them walked by, looked at me and said to his friend, "Hey, Herb, get a load! 'Hee Haw'!" I looked up and the fellow said, "Hey, how you doin' Roy? I watch you all the time on 'Hee Haw.'"

Halsey would always accompany me when I did "The Tonight Show," and while in New York, and later Los Angeles, we'd meet as many people, publishers, and agents as possible. Jim would say, "If we're going to do 'The Tonight Show' on Friday, let's go up to New York on Wednesday." Wednesday, Thursday, and Friday morning we'd go all over New York City meeting every agent, every promoter, every music publisher. Finally, one day I asked Jim why he had me running around all over the city like that, meeting all these people when I could be resting. He said, "We may not be doing business with most of them right now, but we will be down the line. It's a lot easier to call someone on the phone you visited a month before than to call someone you haven't seen for two or three years when you're trying to get a deal going. So we need to keep making these contacts."

It was on one of those trips that Halsey and I went out to dinner at a very nice French restaurant in midtown Manhattan, and although we had reservations we still had to wait five minutes or so. We were standing there when the maître d' came up and in very broken English said, "Your table is reh-dee, and as they say in my countree, Monsieur Clark, 'Hee Haw' . . ." That's when I knew I had really arrived! In spite of what Fred Silverman may have thought, it wasn't only farmers that watched the show.

Because of "Hee Haw," I came to be regarded as one of the top ten most "believable" television personalities. As a result, I got offered a lot of commercials, and did a lot of public service announcements. And, in 1974, I was asked by the producers if I would be interested in hosting "The Tonight Show." Johnny had by this time permanently relocated to the West Coast, and every so often someone would be asked to guest-host.

The invitation came about as a result of Halsey's having gotten together with Fred De Cordova, "The Tonight Show's" executive producer. During the course of their conversation Halsey said, "Hey, I know you have guest hosts on occasion, why don't you consider using Roy sometime?" De Cordova thought about it and said, yes, he thought it was a good idea.

Soon enough, I found myself scheduled to host two consecutive Mondays, after which De Cordova offered me an entire week. Boy, you talk about a hot seat! There's almost nothing harder than hosting "The Tonight Show." You've got to sit there and be intelligent enough in conversation with your guest to bring them out and let them perform, and the more you succeed at it, the more you find yourself having to pull back.

If a guest comes out and says, "Well a funny thing happened to me on the way to the forum," you can't say, "Well, that reminds me, a funnier thing happened to *me* on the way to the forum." You have to say just enough to keep them talking and get them to express whatever it is they want to talk about. And that ain't easy!

Instead of a monologue I would come out, do two songs, an opener, something uptempo, followed by a little dialogue to set up the next song, which would be something special, maybe from my new record. After that, I'd thank the audience and say "Welcome to 'The Tonight Show,' we have Gisele MacKenzie and Peter Lawford on tonight, so stay tuned and we'll be right back." We'd then go to commercial and I'd go over to the desk. Sometimes Ed would be there, but usually when Johnny took off, Ed did also. So Tommy Newsome would lead the orchestra, and Doc Severinsen would be my right hand.

The first night I hosted, by the way, I was sure was going to be my last. My initial guest happened to be only an American institution, the great Mr. Bob Hope. What, I wondered to myself, could I possibly ask him? Gee, Bob, it's nice to see you, how long have you been in show business? I was petrified, but Bob, being a thorough professional, was terrific, and helped me through it. He said some nice things about me on the air that night. At one point he just leaned back and said, "You know, you have a face like an open fireplace. There's nothing hidden behind it. Everything that you think or do is shown in your face." Thank you, Bob!

I remember trying to think who I could have on as a guest

that week who would be different, and decided to try Colonel Tom Parker. I called him and he said, "Hey, kid, what's happenin'? How's it goin'?" We chatted for a while, and then he said, "Well, what do you want?" He knew I wanted something, that I wasn't just calling to pass the time of day.

I said, "Well, I'm hosting 'The Tonight Show' for a week and—"

He cut me off before I could say anything else. "Well, Elvis don't do those kind of shows. They don't pay anything. If I did the show I'd have to change the name of my book."

I said, "Oh, you're writing a book?"

"Yes," he said. "It's called, *How Much Does It Cost if It's Free?*" He went on to say that he'd do the show if they let him set up an Elvis souvenir stand in the lobby.

I said, "Wait a minute, Colonel, I don't want Elvis on the show, I want *you.*"

He said, "Aw, kid, I'm harder to get than Elvis! But I do have this dancing chicken act I'll give you!"

In addition to "The Tonight Show," I was fortunate enough to appear on most of the crown jewels of American television network variety programs. I did "The Jackie Gleason Show" several times. I remember flying down to Miami Beach one time to appear along with Roy Acuff as part of a "Jackie Gleason 'Hee Haw' Country Show" special.

Jackie never liked to rehearse, so the first time I actually saw him was in the studio forty-five minutes before we were scheduled to tape the show. Jack Philbin, Gleason's executive producer, had stood in for him during rehearsals. When Jackie showed up, Philbin walked him through the entire show, saying, okay, you come out here after that, and stand right here, and then you introduce Roy Clark, and he'll come from over there and he will read this, and so on. The skit we did that night was a takeoff on "Hee Haw's" "pickin' and grinnin'." During the taping, we improvised little lines back and forth. And, of course, Jackie was brilliant.

During the show, he stood backstage with a glass of Jack Daniel's in his hand, and I marveled at how it somehow managed to stay filled. While he drank, someone I never really noticed would come along and see to it that when he set his glass down it was filled back up.

Just before the actual taping, he came over and said, "Hey, pal, how are you doing, pal," and we had a nice friendly conversation. We were standing in the wings, and they told me to get ready, as I was going to be the first one on the show. Just then Gleason turned to me and said, "I've got to tell you something about my connection with country music. Years ago, when I was just getting started, my agent called me and said he had a booking for me. For two thousand dollars a week. And I think I'm on top of the world, pal, you know what I mean? I'm on top of the world. Two thousand bucks a week. Then I found out, somebody told me that this guy Ernie Tubbs is making two thousand dollars *a night!* And I'm thinking, who is this guy?" I loved Jackie, but you can always tell when someone isn't really into country when they call the great Ernest Tubb "Ernie Tubbs." It kinda gives them away, don't you think?

On the other end of the scale, you might recall that Howard Cosell once tried to do an updated version of the old "Ed Sullivan Show." It was only on a short time, and I was invited to appear one of those weeks. Howard, what can I say about him? He's a case, abrasive by nature, but as the host of a television show he had to try to come off pleasant. That's something I'm afraid he's never quite mastered. No matter how hard he tried to be funny and make me feel welcome, it just didn't work. It was those little things he always said.

I remember when I arrived at the studio, he came up and said, "Well, Roy, how do you like being here in New York to do my show?"

I said, "Well, it's just fine, I love any excuse to get back to the city."

"Good," he said, "I'll bet you've got the nicest dressing room you ever had."

Or, "This is the best suit you've ever seen a person wear, isn't it, Roy," and he'd be talking about his own suit, of course. Or he tried to impress you by introducing famous people as if they were his best friends. I remember the night I was on, two of the Kennedys came by. Howard called me over and made a big deal of introducing me. I don't think they could have cared less that I was there, but Howard wasn't trying to impress the Kennedys. For some reason he was out to impress me. I guess that's why I found that the funniest thing he did on the show, the best bit of comedy material he had, was his attempt to play the genial host.

I also did one of the first Joey Bishop shows. For a while in the late sixties, Joey had a late-night talk show on ABC opposite "The Tonight Show." I probably did that show more than any other. I'll never forget the first time I appeared on it: I delivered the line that got me asked back for a second time.

I was the last scheduled guest that night, and when I was finally introduced, Joey had me come out and sit with him at the desk because there was no more room on the couch. No sooner did I sit down than he began apologizing for not having me on sooner. Then he said, "Where are you going from here, Roy?"

I said, "I'm going to New Jersey to play background music for a gas war." Well that just about destroyed him! He sat there with that look on his face while the audience went crazy! Then he said something, I came back, got another big laugh, and he said, "Can you stay over and be on the show tomorrow night?" That's how those things happen to me sometimes. Completely unplanned, a spontaneous one-line throwaway that can make all the difference in the world.

I did "The Ed Sullivan Show" several times, "The Bell Telephone Hour," "This Is Tom Jones," and "The Muppet Show" in London. It just so happened that Jim Henson, the creator of the Muppets, went to Northwestern School in Washington, while I was at Chamberlain, and our schools played each other in sports. Jim didn't actually play so I didn't meet him on the field.

However, our paths did cross early on. Channel 4, WRC television in Washington, where I often appeared, had a five-minute show they broadcast just before the evening news featuring Kermit the Frog and a couple of other characters miming a record, usually something by Homer and Jethro. That's when I first became aware of Jim Henson. Years later, before the Muppets really took off, Jim played a character called Rowlf on the Jimmy Dean show. What a genius he was.

I did Flip Wilson's show several times. He was the Bill Cosby of his day, and then he disappeared from the airwaves, something I've never quite understood.

I often appeared as a celebrity player on "Hollywood Squares," and a couple of years ago did a special edition of the show, hosted by John Davidson, in front of six thousand people in New York City. It may not have been the way I planned it, but I finally got to play the Radio City Music Hall!

I also appeared on a special hosted by Liza Minnelli. Now, I'm a big Liza Minnelli fan. Talk about a total professional. She makes an effort to make everyone feel comfortable, from her guest stars to the crew, the camera people, and the technicians.

However, my biggest thrill on TV was the time I got to work with my total idol, Bing Crosby, on one of his great Christmas specials. I flew from Maryland into Los Angeles for the taping. I couldn't get a direct flight and as a result was running late. I got off the airplane and went right to the rehearsal studio on Sunset Boulevard. Les Brown, Bing's orchestra leader, was there, along with some members of the band.

I walked in with my clothes bag over one arm, my guitar under the other, and saw Bing lying on a bench. Mind you, we'd never met. He was just stretched out, resting, while the orchestra rehearsed his charts.

He had a ball cap pulled down over his eyes, and when he heard me come in he raised it to see who it was. "Hey, Roy, how you doin'?" he said in that familiar drawl. My idol! Of all the people I ever wanted to be like, to emulate, Bing Crosby was at the top of the list! He was everything I ever wanted to be, with one of the truly great voices. In my estimation he could sing a song better than anyone who ever lived. When he sang, he made it look so easy. Like that was the only thing he did. Or when he was acting, it was the same thing, as if *that* was the only thing he did.

I'll never forget, we were also supposed to do a duet of "Moon River." Bing and I would get there early, or stay late, to rehearse our parts. This one time we were sitting by the piano, working on the harmonies, when his lovely wife, Kathryn, came into the room. There was a legitimate vocal for me to sing. Understand, all of my life I worked with trios of tenor singers, which allowed me to do a lot of switching of parts. If it got too high for one guy, he could drop down and another could take over. The upside of that type of singing is the production of beautiful harmonies. The downside for me was that I didn't know a legitimate part from Adam.

Well, Bing was trying his best to teach me my part, but the harmony I sang wasn't the harmony written. He sat there, played block chords on the piano, and finally looked up to me after I hit another note I wasn't supposed to, stopped, turned to Kathryn and said, "You know what his problem is? He was raised on that Presbyterian harmony!"

Through the years I've been approached by producers and been sent numerous sit-com scripts for me to star in, most of which I had to turn down because of the enormous time commitment these shows require. In 1967, I did become a semiregular on "The Beverly Hillbillies." That came about after Jim Halsey got to talking one day with Paul Henning, the creator and producer of "Beverly Hillbillies." They came up with the idea of making me one of the cousins from back in the Ozarks. I also played my character's mother on the show, "Big Mama Halsey," who didn't get along very well with Granny.

They also managed to work my music in. Jethro was going to

be my manager, except he was into rock and roll, wearing peace medallions and long hair, while I was a local yokel hillbilly from the backwoods. The only way Jed would give Jethro any money for his management operation was if he took me on as a client. We had a lot of fun with that set-up.

Finally, "Hee Haw" made it possible for me to sign a million dollar contract with the Hughes chain in Las Vegas, and for fifteen years I headlined at the Sands, the Frontier, and the Desert Inn. Although I never met him, they tell me that one time Howard Hughes actually came in to see me perform.

It's quite a feeling to have your name up in those Las Vegas lights. There's nothing to compare. It's an exciting place in every way. And, of course, Barbara would always come out to Vegas to see the show, usually for the closing week.

For all the good things that came with my success, as the years went on I found for the first time in my life, I had to start thinking about my personal security. I had to put a gate up around our house, because people started driving there, four hundred miles just to see the place. Some would just drive right up and, being country, want to have a picnic.

Some were very hard to deal with, like a family with a seventy-five- or eighty-year-old mother who loved me from television, who drove her three hundred miles to meet me. What do I do? I was on TV every week saying, "Hi, I'm Roy Clark and welcome to 'Hee Haw.' " People would watch and naturally think, boy, old Roy, he's sure a nice guy. That's not ol' Roy the star, that's ol' Roy the regular country boy.

It's something you just can't buy at any price. As big as Frank

Sinatra is, I doubt any people who see him say, "Hey, that's ol' Frank, hey, Frank, how you doin'?" It's something you either have or don't, you can't buy it, you can't create it, and you certainly can't fake it. And I guess it's worth a fence or two now and then. The time you have to worry, I figure, is when you no longer need the fence!

From Tulsa to the Volga

7

With the continuing success of "Hee Haw," I found myself ever more in demand to make personal appearances and play concerts. By the early seventies, I was touring constantly, and I began to feel the physical strain. One day Halsey came to me and said, "You know, Roy, if you lived in the Midwest, you'd get twenty-five or thirty more days at home than you do now with the same schedule."

He was right. Even though I had lived my whole life on the East Coast, in the Washington/Maryland/Virginia area, my tours always began and ended out West. I'd invariably lose one day going out at the start and another coming back home at the end. If I lived in the middle of the country, Halsey pointed out, I would have easier access to both coasts as well as to the North and South.

He'd been after me for a while to move to Tulsa, where he lived. I'd played there a lot, and loved it. Like D.C., it's a big city with a small town personality. I got to thinking about it. From the time my family first moved to Washington, really, in January 1942, until now, the District and its surrounding area had always been my home. I was raised, schooled, and started playing music there. Maybe, I wondered, the time had come to make a change.

In 1974, I went up to see a friend of mine, Wayne Creasy, who lived in Tulsa. He took me out to see his house, a real beauty built in 1929 at the beginning of the depression. I said to Wayne, "Boy, if I could find a big, beautiful house like this, I'd move to Tulsa in a minute." He said okay, he'd look around for one.

About a month or two later he called and said, "Hey, Roy, I think I found you a home." He was talking about the old Titus Mansion in the grandest part of Tulsa, a half block from one of J. Paul Getty's many houses. In addition to being one of the original stockholders of Standard Oil, Titus had independently sunk 180 oil wells during the boom years, 176 of which produced oil. His mansion, Creasy said, was a proper reflection of his success.

I promised that on my next trip out West I would stop off in Tulsa and see the house. I did just that, and it took my breath away by its magnificence! It had thirty-nine rooms, eleven fireplaces, each one made with a different marble taken from all parts of the world, spiral staircases, gold fixtures in the bathrooms, huge walk-in cedar-lined closets, and a built-in pipe organ. Each bedroom was a suite, complete with dressing room and separate bath.

The house had been built between 1929 and 1931, at a cost of one million, three hundred thousand of *those* dollars. It originally sat on ten acres, which were subdivided in the mid-fifties. It had a swimming pool, tennis courts, a five-car garage a city block down from the main house, with living quarters built on top.

I was completely blown away by the whole thing. However, I knew that sometimes what a man likes, a woman may not, so I called Barbara and told her I'd found what I thought was a beautiful house, and asked her if she would take a look at it. I went on to California as she flew to Tulsa. I called her afterwards and she agreed it was absolutely gorgeous. Nothing else we saw even came close. After a lengthy negotiation, I was able to strike a deal and bought it.

Naturally, the first thing we did with this thirty-nine-room mansion was to add three rooms! Barbara wanted a separate dressing area, so we decided to have one built. The house also needed a complete repainting and surface restoration. Over the years, a lot of things had been done to it that were hard to understand. You could tell by the quality of the craftsmanship that the workers who had originally built the house put their hearts into it. That's why we couldn't understand how come every room was painted a variation of green, or why the beautiful moldings were covered in solid colors, rather than being left in their original gold leaf.

Another major problem was no central air-conditioning. Every wall, even those between rooms, was constructed with cement and steel mesh, which made the installation of air ducts a major job. I believe I spent more on that one job than the cost of my three previous homes combined!

We also put in a modern kitchen. The one that was there was quite lovely, but seriously antiquated, like something out of an old hotel, complete with heavy porcelain appliances.

And then, of course, there was the problem of furnishing. When the movers arrived from Maryland, everything we owned fit in the front foyer just inside the door. In the beginning I'd come off the road, walk through the front door, and feel like I'd stepped into a big barn! There was no furniture, other than what we had put in the library, where we spent most of our time, and a bed. I finally said to Barbara, "Go to Sears! Buy a bedroom set on sale! Buy a dining room table! Buy something!"

She always looked at me when I said things like that as if I was crazy. She'd then say, calmly, "You don't do that." She became quite involved, read all kinds of books on how to furnish a home properly, and worked closely with a professional decorator. Barbara says she received a complete education in the field, as good as one she would have gotten had she gone to college and majored in interior design.

Sometimes we'd go on long trips just to purchase one item. Several times we went to Chattanooga and Atlanta to buy antiques. Every once in a while we'd go on a spree, and maybe buy enough furniture to fill a huge moving van, then when it was delivered, we'd look around and say, where did it go? The house would just swallow everything right up. Now if we ever move, it's going to take a small army to do the job. It's hard to believe how much furniture we put into our home!

It took more than two years to finish the renovations, and another three to complete the furnishing. It was an intense five years, and when it was over, Barbara went through a very bad period. We both believe part of it was an artistic postpartum, as in, what do I do now?

It was strange, because after spending so much time creating this wonderful home environment, Barbara realized all over again what I've known about her since the day I first met her, that she's not a typical housewife. She doesn't enjoy going to the store, or doing the cooking and the ironing. She needs to be involved in outside projects.

At the same time, Barbara has never wanted to be in the spotlight. She prefers being the woman behind the man. For a long long time, she didn't even want to go to functions with me if they were going to make a to-do about her. If I was going to be on television, if there were going to be cameras there, she'd prefer to meet me after the ceremonies. She's overcome that, and will now at least sit on a dais.

Make no mistake, I greatly appreciate the fact that she is and always has been there for me one hundred percent. She's also my biggest fan. Barbara will sometimes come to my show six nights a week and sit there in that audience and applaud and laugh at everything I do. I'll tell her after that she doesn't have to come every night, she's seen and heard all my songs and *schtick* a million times, but she says she still likes it, and still loves seeing me perform. What a woman!

After thirty-seven years together, I can say there's a lot of things I wish had been different between us. I wish that neither one of us had had a previous marriage, that we had been the first for each other. I wish we could have had children together. I wish I could have been around the kids more. And most of all, I wish this business was such that we could have spent more time together.

On the other hand, the necessary separations have, through the years, made our relationship stronger and healthier. It taught us how to tolerate each other more and to make those moments we do have together better to compensate for all that time we were apart. It taught us to cling to each other a little tighter, and to say out loud how much we love each other, rather than taking it for granted.

One thing that really helped get Barbara out of her depression was a growing involvement in the church. Oral Roberts is based in Tulsa, as is Kenneth Hagen, of the Rhema Bible School. Both men have become very important to us. Barbara took a course at the Rhema Bible School, the same course that ministers take. Tulsa awakened in her something that reached all the way back to her childhood, a kind of calling, I guess, toward the church. She's been actively involved with the Bible school now for more than fifteen years.

Christianity is the biggest thing in our lives. I've heard Barbara say many times that her discovering the Rhema Bible School didn't just happen, that the origins of it go all the way back to her childhood. When she was growing up, church wasn't a big part of her life. On Sunday mornings, there was a little church not far from where she lived. She would find herself on the outside, listening to them singing inside, and knew there was something inside pulling her toward that. For years she kept that urge to find out what it was all about bottled up inside of her; then she finally discovered Rhema. Once she got involved there, she just couldn't get enough of it. As a result, she has become a complete person. The part of her that was missing has now been filled in the most beautiful way possible.

Shortly after we moved to Oklahoma, I had the unique opportunity to travel to and perform in the Soviet Union. In fact, we left on the trip while we were still living in Maryland and returned to take up residence in our home in Tulsa.

Without a doubt, Russia was among the highpoints of my career. How it came about was, late in 1974, I was working in Las Vegas the same time a group of Soviets from all the different Republics were visiting the United States as part of a cultural exchange. I believe they were farmers, doctors, and scientists here to study our farming methods and tour some of our laboratories.

Jim Halsey happened to read an interview in the newspapers with one of the Soviets. He was asked if there was anything the group wasn't going to get a chance to see that they would like to. He said almost every one of them wanted to see Las Vegas.

Well, the lightbulb came on over Halsey's head. He went to the management of the Frontier Hotel, where I was appearing, and asked if Roy Clark invited the group to Las Vegas, would they put them up? The Frontier thought it would be great publicity for them, and said of course they would. In addition, upon their arrival, the hotel gave each Soviet a twenty-five-dollar bag of chips to gamble with. "Oh boy," I said to Halsey, "we'll surely Americanize these Russians in a hurry!"

Their first night in Las Vegas we threw a big cocktail party for them. They saw my show, they gambled, took in the sights and had themselves a ball. As the visit came to an end one of the leaders of the group came to me and said how much they appreciated being invited to Las Vegas, and would I like to come to his country. "Would I? I'd love to," I told him.

There followed a solid year during which details were worked out between our government and theirs for what became, in effect, the second phase of a joint cultural exchange. There was no money involved, no fees paid of any kind. The American government agreed to pay our way to Russia, the Soviet government agreed to pick up our expenses while we were there, and fly us home. It was also agreed that all revenues from the ticket sales of our concerts would remain with the Soviet Union. We also hoped to be able to videotape the show, but ultimately couldn't due to a massive amount of, ahem, "red tape."

In addition to my regular band, I decided to take the Oak Ridge Boys with me. At the time, they were not doing so well—just about surviving, really—and were seriously thinking of giving up on their attempt to cross over from gospel to pure country. Things had gotten so bad for them they couldn't make their payroll. I lent them some money to get through, no big deal, and gave them as much moral encouragement as I could. I believed in them and kept telling them over and over again, hey, you guys are on the brink. Their problem was, in making the transition, they had lost much of their gospel following and hadn't as yet gained enough country fans. As a result they were really disheartened. I decided to take them on the Russia trip as a way of boosting their morale. Which is not to say they weren't a great addition to our show.

We had several meetings with our State Department, during which we were told what to do and what not to do while we were in the Soviet Union, where we could go and where we couldn't, which invitations to accept—there would be very few—and which we had to turn down. And above all, we were warned, we shouldn't wander around alone at night. If we intended to go anywhere in the evenings, we had to be sure to let someone know where and what time we expected to return.

When the tour finally began, in January of 1976, a fellow from the State Department met up with us in Las Vegas, which had become our official point of departure. The group flew from Las Vegas to Tulsa, and then on to Washington's Dulles Airport, where we had one more two-hour meeting with the State Department's diplomacy specialists. It was more like a drill, really, going through everything one more time, what to do, what not to do. Once that was completed, we were finally allowed to board a plane to London, where we stayed over-night before continuing the next day to Moscow.

Upon our arrival, we immediately boarded a train bound for Riga, Latvia, a two-and-a-half-day journey, in the snowbound dead of winter.

Let me tell you, the Soviet Union was the most foreign environment I ever experienced, by a millionfold. There was no sign of anything that hinted of the outside world. If it wasn't made in Russia, it didn't exist. During our entire stay I saw maybe two or three black Chevrolets at the American embassy. Other than that, everything was Russian. No Mercedeses, no other American cars of any type, no Pepsi, no McDonald's, nothing to remind you that America even existed, except maybe the total lack of anything American.

Everything was gray, including the people on the street. All their clothes were dark. Because it was cold, and because dry cleaning was almost nil, they wore heavy clothes that didn't soil or wrinkle easily, and a lot of furs. People didn't linger on street corners and talk to one another, like we do. Instead they kept their heads down, with grim looks on their faces, always going somewhere. No "Hi, how you doing?" No acknowledg-ment that anyone else was out there.

On the other hand, much to my surprise and delight, when I was able to reach the Russians on a one-on-one basis, they behaved quite differently. It quickly became obvious to me they had been taught Americans were the enemy, that they shouldn't trust them, shouldn't talk to them. Once they got over that and saw that I, an American, was no threat, just a normal person, they soon let their guard down.

We were taken on official guided tours every day. We did a lot of miniconcerts at various conservatories. We performed for them, and, in return, the students played for us. Traditional Russian folk music is a very big thing in the Soviet Union, and the people and students recognized American country music as its counterpart. Keeping Russian folk music alive was a state-designated directive. "We will revive and keep our folk music alive and you are designated not only to learn to play this old instrument, but you will research it and build one and learn to play it." That kind of thing.

At times I wondered how the Russian people knew about me, which they obviously did, and why they were interested in my music. I found out that before our tour, some shows and interviews I'd done for the Voice of America, in which I played a lot of my music and told a lot of my history, were aired over and over again. Back then, the Soviets were still blocking the Voice of America, but they allowed those broadcasts through. So by the time we got there, the Russians were waiting for us! For the first time, I thought I understood what it must have been like when the Beatles invaded America!

We did a total of sixteen shows in eighteen days. We played a lot of ice arenas and auditoriums that seated thousands of people. Some of the audience were government officials, with ribbons all over their chests, who were given free tickets. The rest were people of all ages who had come to see us. Every show was sold out, and tickets were being scalped in Moscow for something like 160 rubles, or two months' wages for the average worker. That's how much the Russian people wanted to see an authentic American country music show. They were into three things American—country music, jazz, and the history of the West. Talking with them, I realized they thought Indians and cowboys still roamed the prairies.

I also got the feeling they would have killed or sold their firstborn for a hamburger. We would get these cans of Pepsi-Cola from the American embassy, take them to the dressing room, and put them up in the windows to keep cool. There would always be three or four guys on the outside, waiting for their chance to reach up and grab them. You'd see a hand suddenly, and then, POW, that can was gone!

I did a lot of Russian television while I was over there. I did some of their biggest shows, and found that, except for their use of the European system of high quality color, their technology was quite primitive. On May Day, their equivalent of our Fourth of July, we did three TV shows. It was the first time an American act had ever been allowed inside a Soviet television studio. There had been other American acts on Soviet TV, but they always had been filmed outside, on location, never actually in a Russian studio. We were told that literally everyone who had access to a television set in the Soviet Union would see us, because the shows we did were continually rebroadcast.

The more concerts and TV we did the better they got. We really began rolling after the first couple. The masses supposedly spoke no English, although we found that many actually did, because it's mandatory to study English in school. Our shows proved all over again the cliché I've heard a million times about music, that it *is* the universal language.

I had an interpreter whose first name was Alexander, followed by a long, unpronounceable Russian surname. I simply called him "Shuda." He had studied American cinematography, so he was more "Americanized" than most Russians we came into contact with. At the start of every concert, I would be introduced by Shuda, in Russian of course. Before singing and playing, I'd call Shuda back out and do some *schtick* with him.

Shuda had a boyish face that made him look somehow old and young at the same time. His eyes would twinkle when I did my stuff, the gar-*bage* off the top of my head. At first I stayed pretty straight, but when I saw he was picking up on it, I really started playing with him.

Whenever I would start to ad-lib, his eyes would get bigger. He'd look at me, pause a beat, and then repeat in Russian what I had said. I'd tell him a joke, he'd look at me, the band would break up, and then he would repeat it for the audience. Most didn't know what I had said until Shuda told them, so we'd wind up getting two or three reactions to every joke we did. What was so neat about Shuda was his ability to take all my American slang and turn it into Russian slang, so the audience didn't miss a thing.

The last day of the tour, the government ran a full-page feature on us in their newspaper, *Pravda,* the whole back page, with photos of us, telling the people who we were, what we had done, and where we had played. We were told by our side that this was absolutely unprecedented. If *Pravda* ever mentioned anything like this at all, it was usually long after the fact, a small blurb near the back of the paper. A representative from the American embassy told us we had accomplished something that would, one day, make other things previously unheard of in the Soviet Union possible.

While in Moscow, we stayed at the Rossia Hotel in Red Square, directly across from the Kremlin. On the morning we were ready to begin the long journey home, we had to go through the usual formalities, reclaiming the passports we had surrendered at check-in and making sure all our bills were paid. Only after that was done were we finally allowed to leave.

It was before dawn, still pitch black when we boarded buses

to take us to the airport. With snow spitting in the dead of winter, the Kremlin was lit up, and we could clearly see the Soviet flag, with the star, hammer, and sickle, all waving reddish hued against an ebony black sky.

We were taken to the airport and boarded our plane for Paris. There we had a two-hour layover, before continuing on a direct flight to Dulles Airport, just outside of D.C., where buses were waiting to take us into Washington proper.

And so, within one fourteen-hour time frame, we had literally made the journey from enslavement to liberty. We had left the Kremlin and arrived in the Land of the Free. I remember the exact moment our bus turned a corner and for the first time since we'd been away we could see the Capitol, *our* Capitol, and Old Glory waving, lit up against another pitch black sky. After three weeks in the Soviet Union, everybody in the bus just jumped up and, with tears flowing down our faces, started singing "God Bless America."

In 1988, we made another trip to the Soviet Union. Our first tour had been such a success, we had made so many friends over there, they had been after us for some time to come back. When we finally did, my first impression was that the twelve years that had passed between trips felt more like twelve hundred. There was a totally different atmosphere now. Everywhere we went, people talked openly of love and world peace. In 1976 we had seen no churches, although I'm told there had been a few around, which the government permitted older people to attend. Young people, however, could get into serious trouble if they were caught inside. I guess the Soviet government tolerated the old people and their old ways, figuring they'd die off soon enough. In 1988, though, the churches were open and filled with people of all ages.

In the intervening years, we had taken our show to Bulgaria, Belgium, England several times—you name the country, we played it—until finally we were able to make our grand return to the Soviet Union. This time we did it as a commercial venture, without either government sponsoring us.

Halsey worked out a deal to have the show commercially backed, in a joint venture with a private Soviet talent agency, although everything there was still supposed to be "official." Halsey worked with the Soviet promoter to overcome all the obstacles. The most difficult problem was money. Rubles couldn't be taken out of the country and had no value on the international money exchange. Eventually two accounts had to be kept, a ruble account and a dollar account. A deal was worked out so the money from ticket sales was equally divided into rubles and dollars.

Our biggest asset was the syndicated American television special we made of the trip. We took a film company with us from America, Jim Owens Productions, out of Nashville. Lorry Anne Crook, Jim's wife (of TNN's "Crook and Chase" television program), came along. Earlier in her career she had studied Russian, hoping to be a foreign correspondent. Her fluency in the language was a valuable asset to us, as several times she introduced us on stage in Russian, which the audiences loved.

I was constantly miked, and because the crew were so un-obtrusive, I sometimes forgot I was being taped. In one of the last days we were there, David Hunt, the lead cameraman, and one of the directors came up to me and said, "Roy, give us a break, we're trying to get a television show out of this, would you say something that makes sense?" That's how laid back we all were. Jim Owens's people did an incredible job. They really captured on video the way it was. The show has been broadcast several times, and was very successful.

I have to say, though, that someone sure dropped the ball on us. They promoted the airing of the special well enough, but they didn't promote the show in the Country Music Academy's annual award category of country music documentaries. We weren't even nominated, and we were such an obvious choice. Along the way, someone sure needed a calf puller to get his head out of his own behind!

When we returned from the second Russian tour, Halsey and I began talking about where next to go. I made the comment that the only other place on this planet I could think of that might be more fun than Russia to perform in would be Red China. What a challenge that would be. In Russia we at least resembled one another. In China I'd be in a completely alien culture, where people not only were physically unlike me but behaved completely differently from anyone I'd ever known. Even their music was completely different, with notes and chord structures most Americans have never even heard of.

Halsey began making the appropriate contacts with the Chinese embassy, and sure enough, we got a lot of interested feedback from them. We then started making serious plans to go, until all of a sudden everything came to a screeching halt. The Chinese did an about-face, and said they had no interest in my coming to their county, even as a tourist. I later found out that when we first made contact with them, they had been unaware of my trip to Russia. Once they found out about that, they thought the Soviets and I were big buddies and therefore didn't want us coming into their country.

That, of course, was precisely the kind of political thinking I have absolutely no interest in. My only purpose in wanting to make these trips in the first place is to bring people together, not to polarize them. I still hope to go to China someday, and show them that in spite of whatever differences may exist between our governments, we are all citizens of the same planet, all brothers under the skin.

And most important, all children of God.

Horses, Bikes, and Planes

8

I have always loved flying. I was one of those all-American kids born with the desire to fly high and fast. I can remember being five years old and already fascinated by airplanes. I was mesmerized the first time I heard the sound of an airplane in the sky. I couldn't see it but I could hear it, many minutes before it finally came into view. I remember sitting, waiting, seeing it as it came over the horizon, and then watching it fly out of sight.

During those years, the Second World War was raging, and there was a lot of romance and glamour associated with flying, especially for young boys like myself. It was possible to send away to cereal companies for little cardboard cockpits you would hook up to the controls and footpedals with strings.

In Meherrin, the town where I was born and raised, the main industry was lumber. There were lots of sawmills, saw-dust piles, and all kinds of discarded woods, including strips of heavy oak. When I was eleven, my cousin Waymon and I used to go down to the yards and collect them. One day we decided to build a glider out of the stuff. We went into the slab pile, laid out some strips of oak, and nailed together enough pieces to make a pair of wings. We then made part of a fuselage, and eventually planned to "borrow" bedsheets from our home to cover the whole thing. It's a good thing we never actually finished, or we surely would have both been killed. The thing would have weighed eleven or twelve hundred pounds, and our plan was to get airborne by pushing our "plane" off the top of a cliff!

As soon as I was old enough, I got into motorcycles. I'm still into them to this day; I own several, and ride whenever I can. In 1949, while I was still in high school, I bought my first bike, that 1941 Indian Chief. It became my only mode of transportation. I rode it in sleet, snow, wind, rain, whatever. Then, in 1954, I bought my first Harley-Davidson, and in 1956 my first new motorcycle, a Harley KHK, for which I paid nine hundred dollars. Besides providing me with transportation, I used it to compete in hill-climbs. That same bike today is called a Sporters Harley and sells for eleven thousand dollars.

At the time I couldn't afford what I really wanted, the big 74 Electraglide. I could have bought one then, fully dressed, for fifteen hundred dollars. They now go for fifteen, sixteen thousand dollars!

I eventually sold the KHK and went without a bike for several years. My career was starting to move and I didn't have time to think about motorcycles until the mid-sixties, when I got the urge again, about the same time that I got seriously into flying.

All during my biking days, my fascination with flying stayed with me. One night in the spring of 1956, while I was playing in one of the Washington clubs, an off-duty D.C. policeman by the name of Bill Smith came in, and during one of my breaks we got to talking. Pretty soon flying came up. He said he was a pilot, and before the night was over he offered to teach me how to fly. My fascination with planes mirrored his with the guitar, so we each had an excuse to get closer to the other's field of expertise.

He belonged to a flying club located in Virginia, and, as he said he would, he started giving me lessons. He wasn't really an instructor, but he did get me my requisite air time, and a friend of his, Chuck Fox, who was an airline pilot and had an official instructor's rating, signed my log book.

I would work all night in clubs then get up early the next morning to fly with Bill. To be truthful, a lot of mornings after I had done a little too much partying the night before, I just didn't feel up to it. On those days his advice to me was always the same. If I was going to learn how to fly, I had to make a real commitment to it. I knew what he meant. There was no difference, I realized, between learning how to fly and learning to play the guitar. There is just no substitute for discipline.

So I crossed the line and promised myself I would give it a fair shake. We spent a lot of time after that up in the air, and sometimes our experiences were less than, shall I say, exhilarating? I lived in Maryland, and Bill was based in Fairfax, Virginia. One time we agreed he would pick me up in his PA 14, a Piper four-seater airplane with two side-by-side sticks, at a little airport in College Park, Maryland, right next to the university.

Well, I had had a really rough night. I was in the left seat, the pilot's seat, and as we climbed into the air, I still felt a little woozy. It just so happened a building was being constructed at the end of what was a very short runway. The steel work was up about two stories, and a couple of workers were on top of it. We did some stalls, and when it was time for me to land the plane, I came in sloppy, a little too fast and high.

As I approached the runway, I found myself still fifty feet in the air, with the runway quickly disappearing behind me. Because I had built up too much speed I wasn't losing altitude. Halfway down the runway I was still twenty feet off the ground, and knew I had to go around and make another approach. However, before I could get the throttle in, Bill reached down to shift the landing flaps to go-around flaps, and the stick slipped out of his hand. The landing flaps went full-up and we hit that runway like a ton of bricks.

The wheels came up, the wing tips came down. Bill yelled, "I've got it!" I looked out, and here was this building at the end of the runway, with those two guys on top of a steel beam staring at us coming right at them. One of the men started waving his arms and shouting, "No, no, don't, no, don't come any further . . . no . . ."

Bill finally yanked the stick, and we quivered and shook as we went up the side of that building. When I looked down there was nobody on the steel beam. And there was no ladder. The two men had jumped for their lives!

In spite of that little mishap, I kept at it and by 1957 became a good enough pilot to solo for the first time. I flew pretty regularly for about three years after that, until 1960, when I went out on the road with Wanda and lost my easy access. With Bill, all I had to do was pay for fuel, which was very cheap then, something like thirty cents a gallon.

I got seriously back into flying about 1967. I was doing pretty well, had a little money, and decided to renew my student license. I thought all I had to do was go out and rent an airplane the way I did a car. Well, after doing that two or three times, and experiencing the endless hassles attached to what I thought was going to be a simple procedure, I decided it was going to be much easier just to buy my own airplane.

So I purchased a little tri-pacer, which, by the way, I still have. A tri-pacer is a basic four-seater Piper, with tricycle landing gear, one of the first truly affordable four-place airplanes available to the general public. It's capable of flying about a hundred twenty miles an hour, up to five hours on a tank of gas. It's a perfect plane to experience the sport of flying.

Shortly after I bought it, I got my full pilot's license and, a couple of months after that, decided to invest in a slightly bigger plane, a straight-tail Beechcraft Debonair. That became the first plane I used for business. The range is about nine hundred miles, perfect for touring. I used the Debonair for a couple of years, and then moved up again, this time to a twin-engine Cessna 310, a nifty, fast little airplane capable of doing a hundred eighty knots, with the added safety advantage of twin engines.

At this point I got to thinking, with the schedule I had, and the amount of flying I was doing, I didn't want to be up in the air in marginal weather thinking about a job I have to go to or one I just did, attempting landings in congested terminal areas. I decided the time had come for me to hire a full-time pilot. In that way, I could retain the pleasure of flying, while having someone else take care of all the paperwork, maintenance, and servicing of the aircraft.

When you get as serious about flying as I did, you're always chasing speed. The faster you go, the faster you want to go, and the faster it makes sense you should go. I guess that's the real reason I decided my next upgrade would be to a Mitsubishi

MU2, a turboprop twin engine capable of cruising up to thirty thousand feet at a speed of three hundred miles per hour. Not long after, I traded it in for the J stretch model, which went about the same speed but with a lot more interior room. Then, in 1979, I bought a new Marquis, which was the top of the line MU2. It had big engines, was very fast, and could fly long distances at an altitude of thirty-six thousand feet.

I stayed with the Marquis for five years, until it got to a point where I had to put some serious money into the prop jet turbine engines, which are very expensive to maintain. You have to understand that all my life I've been an impulse buyer. If I saw something and wanted it, I wanted it *now*. I never liked to wait until tomorrow, which was something my accountants have always tried, without much success, to teach me how to do. So when they came to me and said it made better sense to buy a "pure" jet rather than to maintain the Marquis, I jumped at the idea. I went right out and bought a Mitsubishi Diamond lA.

The Beechjet, as it's popularly known, requires two pilots up front at all times. It therefore became very involved for me to get type-rated in it. I had to stay current, which meant every six months going back to flight safety school, followed by a proficiency check, which took about a week. Every time the airplane went somewhere I either had to go along or hire another pilot.

Now I had two full-time pilots, and quadruple the expenses, because of insurance and additional road costs. Maintenance fees were enormous and it seemed, as with every precision instrument, something always went wrong. The problem is, any little thing that has to be attended to on a pure jet is a major expense. I remember one time Conway Twitty lost the fuel cap from his Jet Commander, a little piece of aluminum that screws in where you pump your fuel. You have one on your car. The cost of a new one? Four hundred dollars! Windshields have a tendency to get checkered and have to be replaced. Four thousand dollars. And that's just for one side, thank you very much!

After two and a half years, the same accountants who had urged me to buy the jet told me I could no longer afford to keep it. Looking back, I think if they hadn't had talked me into getting it, I would still be flying my Marquis. Nevertheless, after twenty-eight years of constant flying, once I sold the jet, I decided it was far more cost effective to turn to buses for my primary mode of business travel.

Obviously, surface transportation, no matter how luxurious, is a totally different world. To me, airplanes had become a necessity rather than a luxury. When I had the jet I could leave home at four o'clock in the afternoon, fly to a job seven hundred miles away, do the show, return to the airport and be back in my own bed by two o'clock in the morning. Once I sold it, that kind of convenience was gone. With a bus, even though there are a lot of times you have a day off between engagements, you still can't go home, so you wind up staying out on the road.

Recreational flying is still a very big part of my life. It's an old but true cliché that when the wheels leave the runway so do all your problems. I still have three airplanes, including a turbo 210, single engine, a 165-knot little airplane. I've gone to Virginia from Tulsa with it on occasion, but it's not really the kind of craft you want to use day in and day out for business.

I also have a Stearman open cockpit, double-wing biplane. One day I'd just like to get into it, take off and go on a barnstorming tour. My fantasy is to get up every morning and only then decide where I want to fly to that day. I'd spend the night under the wing in a sleeping bag, get up early the next morning, take off, and, whenever I felt like it, set her down.

My interest in aviation has provided me with some incredible experiences. I have been privileged to fly with the Tulsa Air National Guard. We spent four hours training ejection parachute maneuvers on the ground. When we finally went up we broke the sound barrier.

However, without question, the most amazing time I've ever had in the air was when I flew with the Blue Angels. Mind you, I'm one of those guys who still gets a lump in his throat when he sees the American flag and hears "The Star-Spangled Banner" at ballgames. To me, the living embodiment of that kind of patriotism is the naval flying team the Blue Angels.

The Blue Angels are, essentially, a public relations operation, intended to help maintain support for the navy. They are all young men at the top of their game, without question the finest pilots in the world. They can only be a team member for two years, during which time all they do is fly and train. When they're not working on maneuvers, they spend half their day flying and half their day physically working out.

What happened was, I was playing Reno in 1981, the same time the Reno air races were scheduled, which that year featured the Blue Angels. It just so happened the pilots were fans of mine, and one night they came down to John Asquaga's Nugget to see me play. We got to talking, I told them about my own flying experience, and before I knew it I was invited to go up with them!

What an absolute kick! I went up early the next morning in the #7 plane, an F-4 Phantom jet, the only two-seater in the squadron. I flew with Captain Kenneth Miller, and we did every maneuver the Blue Angels perform in their show.

I was in the back and Kenneth was in the front. He knew that I was a pilot, and through the head gear, he suddenly said, "Roy, do you want to fly it?"

I said, "I'd love to!"

"Okay," he said, "you got it. Give me a ninety degree turn to the left and hold your altitude."

I did.

"Now give me a turn a hundred and eighty degrees to the right and hold your altitude."

I did.

"You have a nice touch," he said.

Well! If you don't think I didn't swell up! Then we did maneuvers. He did a loop, a roll-out on top, then he let me try it. He talked me through, then showed me the roll. The F-4 is capable of doing two complete rolls in a single second. He told me to brace myself, which I did, but my head still hit the canopy!

I flew it all over the airbase, and when it was time to return, Kenneth landed us. The only thing that really bothered me was the same thing that had bothered me when I flew with the Tulsa National Guard. As the crew chief strapped me in, he told me what this one handle was for. "When you're not flying, the rudder pedals are here," he said, "and you put your feet back in the stirrups. That's the position you're in to eject. If your legs are out of position and you attempt ejection, you won't have any legs left. They'll be sheared right off at the knees by the instrument panel." *Uh-huh.*

He then added that when I reached down and pulled the pin out, the seat was armed for ejection. *That meant I was sitting on a live charge.* "So don't push this button . . . if you have to go out, he, the pilot, will jettison the canopy and send you out first, then come out behind you. You won't have to do anything, if it should come to that." *If it should come to that!* I swallowed hard and said I understood.

The pilots all came back to the club the next night and made me an honorary ground-crew member, only the second one in Blue Angel history, *ahem,* and the first civilian to be so honored. It was actually against standard regulations, so all the officers had to turn their backs, with a smile on their faces of course, while this honor was bestowed on me.

About a year later, I was invited to emcee the National Aviation Hall of Fame awards, in Dayton, Ohio, where I had the privilege of meeting Senator Barry Goldwater and the legendary Jimmy Doolittle. I made what I thought was a cute remark to General Doolittle at the cocktail party before the ceremonies. He was late getting there because he lives out of San Diego and one of his flight connections missed. I said, "General, why didn't you just rent an airplane and fly on in." He was eighty-nine years old at the time and I was being a bit facetious. He just looked at me and said, "Well, Roy, I've already done all I want to do in flying. There's nothing else I care to do." I said, "Ah, yes, yes, of course, sir, I understand, sir."

The Blue Angels were also there, the same crew, the same pilot I had flown with. These were now my buddies! My friends!

The next day I went out to the air show, and the Blue Angels dedicated their flight to me. There I was, inside the ropes right next to the planes, as they went up, did their routines, landed, and taxied to where we were. The canopies went back, they took their helmets off, put their dress hats on, got out of the planes at the same time, went down, shook the hand of their crew chief, thanked him for a good flight, marched away from the airplanes, then suddenly broke rank and ran up and hugged me. What a moment!

One more thing about that day. I had flown my Marquis into Dayton for the event. It didn't dawn on me until much later that I had to leave the next morning and the airport would be closed for the show. I told the leader of the Blue Angels about my predicament, and he suggested I go out with them.

He arranged special clearance for me, and I attended a briefing session with the boys. There I was, just like a regular Blue Angel, listening in as they discussed what they were planning to do that day. We were to take off and fly a heading west of Dayton, seventy-five hundred feet and maintain two hundred fifty knots indicated air-speed, as high as I could go and maintain that speed in my plane, and as low as they could go. Fast for me, slow for them. Then they gave me a radio frequency, and told me to get ready.

Midway through, they stopped the show and the announcer told the crowd the Blue Angels were leaving, and Roy Clark was leaving with them. The seven airplanes with the Blue Angels taxied out, I taxied behind them, and we were off.

I went up, and all of a sudden I got a call on the radio they were coming up on my starboard side. They gave me a heading to fly, seventy-five hundred feet, two hundred fifty knots. I was instructed to hold that heading, and they'd do the rest. Suddenly, I looked out the window and there they were! Everybody was watching the leader, and the leader was coming closer and closer, looking right at me. I could see if he got a decent shave that morning, he was that close! And he just kept coming.

As we flew, they came in close again, and the pilot of the #7 two-seater airplane I had flown in previously started taking photos of the Blue Angels and me. When he finished, the leader came on the radio, and said they were heading for Pensacola and would see me later! Then they peeled off as a squadron, and I went on to where I was going.

About two weeks later, I got a beautiful sixteen by twenty color photograph of me, my airplane, and the Blue Angels, signed by every one of them. Needless to say, it's one of my most treasured possessions.

In 1993, I was invited to go to Langley Air Force Base outside of Norfolk, Virginia, to fly with the first fighter wing in an F-15, which is a top of the line fighter plane. That came about because of the work I'd done with the Air Force Band. I'd gone down to Panama in 1991 and met Colonel Dave McCloud, who is now General Dave McCloud, the squadron leader, and he invited me to fly with the F-15s. What an experience! I actually flew on a mock mission, just as if we were in battle. We pulled six positive G's, and I thought I was going to leave all of my innards in the bottom of the airplane. I flew with Captain Chris Braman, from Missouri. He's going to bring his mother down to see our show. That's when, I hope, I'll get a chance to show him how I soar!

Over the last several years I've also developed an active interest in racehorses. It began in Maryland, which is, of course, a very big racehorse state, Baltimore being the home of the Preakness. I had some friends in the business, and it was through them that I first starting going to the track. I didn't know anything about horses at first, how to handicap them or anything, and to tell you the truth I still don't know a whole lot. I've noticed, by the way, the people who handicap for a living don't either.

Anyway, in 1967, through these friends I met one of the top trainers in the business, King Leatherbury. He was and is very much into claiming horses, which happens to be one of the two best ways to get into the business; the other being breeding. To breed, however, you have to have breeding stock, at least a stud and a mare. Once they produce a foal, you can't race the foal until it's two years old, so to enter the business through breeding takes at least three years.

Claiming, on the other hand, gets you in immediately. The drawback is, to claim a horse, you have to own one. Claiming races are a way of evaluating horses. Let's say you have an expensive horse and I have a cheap horse, and we enter them both in the same race. Chances are awfully good yours will beat mine. To make things fair, he can enter a claiming race. He enters and declares a value on his horse. If it's worth twenty thousand dollars, naturally it doesn't make sense to put him in a claiming race where he might lose him for a stated value of, say, ten thousand five hundred dollars. On the other hand, if I have a two-thousand-dollar claiming horse, I can't put him in the ten-thousand-dollar race. It's going to cost me money to train and feed that horse for a race he has no hope of winning.

If I have a horse that is roughly a ten/five ($10,000/5,000) horse, I want to put him in a ten/five race. However, once you enter him, you always stand a chance of losing him, as another owner or trainer can claim him at the price you've set. When the gate opens, anyone who has put a claim in now owns your horse. If it comes around and wins, the previous owner gets the purse for that race. If the horse comes out, takes two steps and drops dead, the guy who claimed him has just bought himself a dead horse.

Claiming races can range from twenty-five hundred dollars all the way up to one hundred thousand dollars. The idea is to find where your horse fits. If he runs a couple of races and doesn't win, you drop him down. That, of course, is where a lot of hanky-panky goes on. Someone might come in from out of state with an expensive horse and put him in a fifteen-thousand-dollar claiming race, in an attempt to steal the purse. He's taking a risk doing it, because he can lose his horse, and a lot have been lost in just that way.

I got into horseracing through claiming. I bought a horse from a friend of mine who owned a stable, so I could claim. Soon I had eight horses, enough to have one running every week, and I even had some winners. I didn't make any money, but I did get into the sporting end of it.

Horses, I have discovered, are a great mind leveler. I've since gotten into the breeding end, and have actually birthed foals. To see a horse stand up for the first time, thirty minutes after it's born, to watch it start nursing from the mare, to begin to train it as you watch it grow, and then see it run a race . . . *whooaa* . . . that's a kick!

Horses became a major part of Barbara's life as well. In 1978, we were finishing up the renovations on our new house, and she really wasn't into doing much of anything. She hadn't as yet become that involved with the church and was looking for something to fill the missing slot in her life. When she began to show an interest in horses, we talked about buying some land, and maybe starting a horsebreeding farm.

By this time we already had a few horses running in races back in Maryland, and a brood mare in Kentucky. We were into the early stages of breeding horses, but strictly from a distance, nothing hands on. Occasionally, we'd go to Kentucky to visit our horses, and it was on these trips that Barbara learned a lot about why one horse is bred with another to get a certain desired result.

At the time I had a real show horse that had won national

and world titles. I bought it because I thought it would be something nice for Barbara and me to share. Now, prior to this time, she had fingernails six inches long, like a maharajah. Back then it had been something of a fad to wear a diamond in the little fingernail. She had one, and it used to bug me no end.

She couldn't do anything with her nails out to there, even a task as simple as putting the key into a door. And when she'd break a nail it became a major catastrophe. She'd have to drop everything and go to a special person for immediate nail surgery!

When I bought her first riding horse, I noticed she was paying a lot of attention to it. We kept it up at my bandleader Rodney Lay's farm, in Coffeyville, Kansas, and Barbara always wanted to go up there.

When you get a horse, you have to learn to take care of it, groom it, saddle it, and the like. I wasn't about to saddle Barbara's horse for her. I insisted she had to learn to do it by herself. Then one day I noticed her nails were trimmed. I said, "You cut your nails."

She said, "I had to. I couldn't saddle my horse the way they were." It was a big moment for her. She had finally found something that made it worthwhile to trim those nails and take the diamond out of her pinky. She had fallen in love with that animal, which led to her learning how to ride properly. Eventually, she developed a real interest in the breeding of horses.

I understood and encouraged her commitment. Horses are therapeutic. They are living, breathing animals, with personalities all their own, and they can take all your time and energy.

In 1986, we purchased some land about an hour and a half

from our Tulsa home, not too far from Joplin, Missouri, in the northeast corner of Oklahoma. We took down all the old buildings that were there, started from scratch, and built a showplace farm we like to think is on a par with some of the best Kentucky horsefarms.

The farm became a major project for Barbara. We hired an architect, built a farm manager's home with an office and an apartment for us on the top of it, a big barn for hay, and eight outdoor paddocks. Whenever I went out on the road, Barbara would go to the farm. She learned every aspect of the business, from helping to foal out the babies on up. We have about thirty horses now, and our desire, and we both believe in our hearts it will absolutely happen some day, is to have one of our horses win the Triple Crown.

Barbara says she knows that after all her hard work, after shoveling all the horse crap, doing all the foaling, staying up all night long, literally sleeping in the stall because horses somehow always seem to foal at three in the morning, after all that sacrifice, she knows that when we win the Kentucky Derby, when we're all up on the platform with the governor and all the television personalities, all the talk will be, "Famous country and western television star Roy Clark wins the Kentucky Derby." In the background you'll see this lady on her tiptoes trying to look over their heads to see the television cameras! *In spite of herself!*

Branson Is the Buckle

9

It's rare when a fully creative performer is also a discerning businessman. Unfortunately, because of that fact, performers often get "taken," unless they have somebody they absolutely trust to take care of things like bookings, contracts, payroll, expenses, investments, etc. It's not difficult for me to understand the problems of a Wayne Newton or a Willie Nelson. Poor Willie. The IRS really got on him because of that seven hundred and fifty thousand dollar deduction claim he made for his wardrobe.

Seriously, with the kind of money big-name entertainers make, it isn't long before they start living like a "star," buying big cars, their own helicopter, farms, just the kind of thing the IRS looks for. I could write a separate book on the good old IRS. They came after me for a silver deal and a couple of other investments I went into. Originally they claimed I owed something like two hundred thousand dollars, then sat on the case for fifteen years before coming to judgment. When they finally got around to it, interest and penalties had escalated the figure to over a million!

Among my many astute investments, and the main reason I still have the IRS on my case, was the DeLorean automobile. I was one of the original investors, along with Johnny Carson and Sammy Davis, Jr. As a result, the three of us were prominently named in all the lawsuits. Did I lose on the deal? Let me put it this way. I've never won on any "deal" in which I've gotten involved.

Although we all knew each other for years, the three of us got involved with DeLorean separately. I knew Johnny, of course, from "The Tonight Show," and Sammy and I went all the way back to 1963, the first year I played Lake Tahoe. He was one of those people who, when you met him, you felt you'd known him forever. We first met at Harrah's, when I was working the lounge and he was the star in the main room. In fact, I was there the night he made his final payment to the mob. Early in his career, he needed money and the mob gave it to him. Once they did that, of course, they owned him. It took a very long time for Sammy to pay them off. What a party he threw that night!

Through the years I had appeared on Sammy's television show and he had come on "Hee Haw." It seemed like every noncountry performer at one time or another wanted to do "Hee Haw," put on bib overalls and go in the cornfield. Sammy, I'm happy to say, was no exception.

Anyway, in July 1978, I decided to make a major financial investment in the DeLorean. I just felt the car's conception was such a great idea. John DeLorean originally intended to build his car in Puerto Rico. He had found this ex-military base down there with plenty of available space and buildings. He wanted to make automobiles that would sell for thirteen thousand dollars, to compete with the Corvette, which at the time was selling for fifteen thousand five hundred dollars.

For a variety of reasons, the Puerto Rico site suddenly fell through, and DeLorean had to find a new site for his plant. Eventually he settled on Northern Ireland, and promised his investors from that point on everything would proceed on schedule. And everything did, except for one small thing. Because of the relocation, the company needed more money. A lot of time had been lost in Puerto Rico, and now he was going to have to start over, building from the ground up. I wound up having to double my original investment of twenty-five thousand dollars in order to protect what I had already put up, and more after that.

That, of course, was the beginning of DeLorean's downfall. The car John eventually built wasn't the one he originally conceived. Because of economics, he had to make compromises on everything, from the engine to the frame. Originally, the idea was, for safety purposes, to make the frame with a pressed honeycomb design. That was changed to a conventional steel frame. There also wasn't enough time or money to have the engine certified GTO, which had been an integral selling point.

What can I say? The car he finally made wasn't the one we all thought we were investing in. On top of everything, for all my money and trouble, I didn't even get one! When the list price had risen to twenty-five thousand dollars, each investor had the opportunity to buy two for nineteen thousand dollars each. For one reason or another I didn't. Too bad, 'cause they're worth fortunes now. Another shining example of my powerful investment skills!

I also invested in oil wells. A lot of oil wells. That was the thing to do in Oklahoma. I was making money and told by my accountants that in order to protect it I needed to get into tax shelters. How many of those oil wells paid off? Exactly one. It yielded about as much oil as I could have put into the engines of my two DeLoreans. If I had bought them.

Naturally, then, in the early eighties, when the opportunity came along to invest in a theater in Branson, a little town of two thousand people in the Ozark mountains I had barely heard of, I was more than a bit cautious. I've owned a lot of businesses, including recording studios and radio stations, and the first lesson I learned is that, as with most enterprises, you have to be prepared to make a hands-on contribution. You can't invest in a business and hire someone else to run it. It just doesn't work that way.

As I say, I had reservations. However, the more I thought about it, the idea of owning a theater began to appeal to me, *precisely because I could become personally involved with it.* I would not only own the theater, but perform in it as well. For the first time, I'd have a financial stake, as well as creative control over my own destiny. I'd be working in a stable environment, my equipment would be permanently set up, I wouldn't have to pack and unpack after each show, check in and out of hotels, and travel hundreds of miles a day.

Now, I knew I could make more money going out on the road, but once I factored in all the ancillary expenses, it became clear that I could net about the same by staying in Branson. The only unknown seemed to be whether people would come out to see me. Well I figured they always had before, so why would they suddenly stop now?

*   *   *

One of the first things that impressed me when I went down to see Branson, was that it seemed to have all the right ingredients, and I'm happy to say it still does. Along with a physically beautiful countryside, complete with gorgeous natural lakes, there's something else quite special about the place. The people. Branson remains America's capital of family values. One of the first things you realize when you arrive is that it's like stepping back in time, to an America before John F. Kennedy was assassinated. There's no drugs, no crime, you can walk the street at two o'clock in the morning without worrying about being mugged. People who visit Branson are thrilled they can actually leave their cars unlocked.

The prices are extremely reasonable, too. Sixteen dollars will get you into almost any show. Anywhere else, the same ticket would cost upwards of fifty dollars, easy. A lot of the people who come here are on fixed incomes of one sort or another. We get an awful lot of retired people. They can drive their motor homes right onto the parking lots.

Still, for all that, when people ask me why I came to Branson, I'm never really able to tell them exactly what it was that actually made me go ahead. I never said, well, today I'm going to build a theater, it'll have my name on it and be fabulously successful. Branson just kind of happened.

I first became actively involved with Branson in 1981, along with hotel owner Jim Thomas, his son, and Wayne Creasy, my insurance agent and a longtime friend, the fellow who found the house for Barbara and me in Tulsa. At the time, my accountant, Ernie Smith, was looking for solid investments for me. Solid, as in, I wouldn't lose my shirt. Ernie heard from Jim that

187

he was getting ready to build a celebrity theater in Branson, Missouri, and was looking for a gimmick, something to make his theater stand out and be noticed. He decided to make it a dinner theater and book nationally known country talent.

At the time, I was on the road, touring, doing concerts, and, of course, "Hee Haw," when Ernie told me about Jim's invitation to come down to Branson to check things out. The first free day I had I flew down, and my initial impression was that here was a place where the image of "Hee Haw" was alive and well. Jim then showed me the piece of land he had in mind for the theater, a prime location adjacent to the White Water Amusement Park, owned by Silver Dollar City, which was doing, and still does, gangbuster business. Silver Dollar City is a place that takes you back a hundred years, to a time of wagonwheelers, glassblowers, broommakers, potters, blacksmiths, and basic, lovely dulcimer music. Because Silver Dollar City was so popular, thousands of cars passed by Jim's proposed theater site on the way there every day of the season.

The other show business attractions in Branson at the time were mostly authentic Ozark mountain hillbilly acts like the Presleys, the Ballknobbers, the Texans, and the Foggy River Boys, all of whom coupled country music with old school vaudeville and slapstick comedy, right down to comedians with baggy pants and blacked-out teeth.

I went away with lots of good feelings about Branson but was still unable to make up my mind. Actually, it was Rodney Lay, my bandleader, who helped convince me to make the move. He happened to be familiar with Branson, as he had spent his honeymoon there. I have always trusted Rodney's opinion on matters concerning my career. He's been one of my closest friends now for nearly thirty years.

We first met through Jim Halsey, back in 1960. Rodney had a really popular rock and roll band, Rodney and the Blazers, complete with silver lamé jackets and wraparound sunglasses. They did a lot of Sha-na-na type of rock. One night I was doing a show in Independence, Kansas, during the Neawollah Celebration at Halloween (the celebration William Inge based his play *Picnic* on), when Halsey took me to hear Rodney's band, which was playing at a teen dance.

When I saw all this rock and roll choreography they were doing, I turned to Halsey and asked, "Exactly what did you have in mind?" Halsey suggested we play a few dates together, and that's when I found out just how good these boys really were. I started using the band regularly in 1963, and in 1966 I asked them to play on a live album I recorded in Albuquerque, New Mexico.

We ran into each other on the road quite often after that. By the early seventies, Rodney and his band were backing up several major country artists on the road, including Jody Miller, Barbara Fairchild, and Freddy Fender. In 1976, I was booked to play the Oklahoma County Fair, and for some reason the band that was supposed to back me up couldn't make it. Halsey called Rodney at the last minute and asked if he could fill in. Rodney said sure, and asked Halsey for a list of my set songs, and the keys I did them in.

Rodney then went down to Halsey's office himself, made tapes of all of my records and learned them note for note—the kick-offs, the middle parts, the endings, the background singing, everything. When I got together with him to rehearse, I called off the first song and before I could say anything else, Rodney told the band to play it in the key of C. Right on the money! The same thing happened with the second song. At that point I said, okay, we don't have to rehearse anymore, let's just go for it.

When the show was over, I told Rodney I thought he had done a really good job. I'd been fighting strange bands for a long time, and it had been a real treat for me to just get up on stage and not have to worry about anything but my own performance. I told him this was the first time I'd had a band that cared enough to take the trouble to learn my songs ahead of time. We got to talking one day after a show and I said, "I want to ask you something. Would you consider going on the road full-time with me?"

I thought for sure he would turn me down. At this point in his career, he seemed to be settling down in his own life. He had gotten married, bought a country-western store, and started a family. However, as soon as I asked him, his face lit up and he said, "That's what I'm in this business for!"

"Well, okay," I said. "I'm going to hold you to it, you can't change your mind!" In 1976, Rodney and his band joined me full-time and have been with me ever since. It wasn't too long after that he began talking to me about Branson and raving about what a great place it was.

Well, one thing led to another and I decided I wanted to be a partner in the Roy Clark Celebrity Theater in Branson. Jim Thomas arranged all the financing. We took a terrific, well-publicized photo of the shovel breaking ground, and although the construction didn't go as smoothly as everyone hoped, we finally opened in August of 1983.

And were met with a blizzard of problems. To begin with, we were able to realize only two months of revenue, because in those days, Branson's "season" ran from the first of May through the end of October. Now, of course, it's expanded to virtually the entire year, but that took a while to establish.

So there we were, stuck with all these cash calls and construction costs against no revenue. I had to sign additional notes from the bank to sustain the theater until the next season. At that point I said, whoa, wait a minute. I took another look, didn't figure there was going to be enough money generated here for four investors, and exercised an out-clause option I had in my contract. The partnership was dissolved and Jim Thomas and his son took over as sole owners of the theater, paying me for the use of my name. I could still work as many days as I wanted. The big difference now was I could do it all without the bank notes and other responsibilities.

In our second season, we booked Boxcar Willie to play the theater, while I went out on the road. Boxcar looked around, liked what he saw, went across the street and bought a theater for himself.

For Boxcar, Branson was an absolute godsend. Although he was, for the most part, unknown in the states, in Europe he had been a legend for years. I didn't even know him. One time in the early eighties we were taping "Hee Haw" Empty Arms Hotel segments, and I happened to notice this guy in a hobo outfit pushing a wheelbarrow full of suitcases around like a country bellhop. Nobody had told me who he was, he just came and went.

Later that same year, I traveled to England to play the 1984 Wembley Country Music Festival. When I arrived I checked in with the band, asked how the show was going, and when we were due to appear. Rodney just looked at me and said two words. "Boxcar Willie."

I said, "What? Who?"

Rodney said, "Boxcar Willie is what's happening. He was the first one on the show and no one was able to follow him. He tore it up."

I said, "You're kidding. Boxcar Willie?"

"They loved him. They threw babies in the air!" Well, I thought, maybe I could have him come out with me and tell the audience I was a friend of his.

I soon found out what Rodney was talking about. The audience tolerated me but clearly loved Boxcar Willie. I remember I played my heart out and received nice, polite applause, while Boxcar, doing nothing but old standard country tunes, brought the place to its knees.

Back in the States, Branson proved the perfect showcase for Boxcar. He's been there ever since that first time we booked him into our theater, and every theater is the better for it.

Mel Tillis was the second guest act we booked. Now, Mel and I go back so far I can't remember the first time we met. It seems like we've always known each other. When he played my theater, just like Boxcar, he looked around and said, hey, this is a good thing. The next thing we know, he's buying his own theater.

And no one can blame him or anyone else. There's really no other place anywhere quite like Branson. Lately, I understand, Nashville has been trying to do something similar, but I don't think they can pull it off. They're building theaters there, but the difference is that someone with money and property builds a theater and hires someone else to work in it. That's not what Branson is all about. Here the performer builds the theater, owns it, and runs it.

The major complaint from tourists about Nashville is the high cost. They get you coming and going. For a man with a wife and two kids, Nashvllle can be a very heavy ticket. Besides, after Opryland, most places are really glorified bars, and a lot of families don't want to take the kids into that type of environment.

Mel originally opened up where Loretta Lynn is now. Andy Williams is here as well, along with such major leaguers as Wayne Newton, Jim Stafford, John Davidson, Ray Stevens, Louise Mandrell, and Glenn Campbell, all of whom, except for Wayne Newton, worked at my theater first and now have theaters of their own.

Unfortunately, in 1989, Jim Thomas, at the age of sixty-five, suffered a mild stroke. After he recovered, he then came to me and said, "Roy, I missed my kids growing up, I don't want to miss my grandkids. I'm going to retire. Why don't you take the theater over yourself? I'll just sell it outright to you." In the intervening years, he had built a hotel and physically connected it to the theater. My first reaction was, I didn't want to be tied down, but he kept after me.

Then I got to thinking a little more about it. I rolled the pros and cons over in my mind, while Jim kept assuring me he would give me a great deal. I told him I just wasn't sure, because I had been burned so many times in the past. However, one thing led to another, and the deal he offered was so great, that on April 1, 1991, I went ahead and took over sole ownership of the Roy Clark Theater.

That first year, 1991, I played about one hundred ten dates. In 1992 I did one hundred thirty, and in 1993 two hundred, about as many as I'll do in 1994. The more I'm in Branson now the more sense it makes to me. I get to do what I love, and have a say in how I do it.

The performing community is very tight. There's a definite sense of oneness. We're all interested in Branson being as successful as it can be. The manager of my theater, Taylor Seale, and all the other theater managers meet at least once a week to talk over problems that might affect any one of us.

There are always requests for me to do different things with and for the town of Branson. The Ozark Marketing Council is constantly putting together projects they'd like me to participate in. Sometimes I'll go down to Andy Williams's theater to do a promotion in full performing gear for national television. At the end of every performance, you'll always hear the star say, hey, now don't forget Mickey Gilley, Jim Stafford, Ray Stevens, Mel Tillis, the Presleys, there's a lot of great shows in town.

It's unique that you can build a theater anywhere and have enough people to come fill it up twice a day, every day, for six, seven, eight months a year. You couldn't go to any other town and book a theater for two shows a day every day and expect to have a crowd, unless you were very lucky, past the first three or four days. After that you'd be playing to an empty house.

In 1992, one of the most significant events took place. The Jerry Lewis Muscular Dystrophy Telethon decided to broadcast several segments from Branson interspersed throughout the show. That same year George Bush kicked off his reelection campaign in Branson. He's a big country music fan, and his opening line to us was, "This place is a dream come true." In 1993, satellite broadcasting came to Branson, which has given us greater exposure than ever before.

We now have the first option to buy the hotel, and if we don't exercise it, we still have approval of who does buy it. I say we, because in return for all he's done for me through the years, I made Rodney my partner in the theater. I just didn't want him to become like one of those guys back in the clubs in Washington, sixty years old with no future and no security. That wasn't where I wanted to wind up, and I didn't want

Rodney to either. I've tried to look after his interests and welfare, and the band's as well, because these guys have been loyal to me, and loyalty has always been a big factor in my decision making.

I remember the first time I headlined Vegas. Every time the curtain opened it was a full house. Two shows a night. I never once looked out from the side of the stage to see if there were any people out there, but I always had that one fleeting moment when I wondered, what if the curtain opens and there's no one there? What if the world decided one day that they'd seen enough of Roy Clark? I still get that feeling in Branson. Close to showtime, I start looking around at the parking lot to see how many cars have pulled in. Now that I've got a financial nut to make, it gives me a different perspective. It's no longer a matter of is there a full house here for me to entertain, but are there enough people out here to make the payments on this theater, and pay the band, all the people who work here?

From the very first time I came to Branson, I've heard people say it reminds them of Las Vegas, only without the gambling. There's a strip, a lot of lights, and it's in the middle of nowhere. All that's true, but there's something Branson has that Las Vegas surely doesn't. There's a gospel element to every show.

They used to call the South the Bible Belt. Well, if that's true, Branson has to be the buckle. And, to tell you the truth, I hope and pray that never changes. If they removed that part of Branson, the whole thing might very well collapse. A preacher goes out and shakes hands at the end of his service. The artist here in Branson does the same. Accessibility is a prime ingredient in Branson's success. If a performer doesn't go out, meet the audience and sign autographs, and have pictures taken with them, they won't be satisfied, no matter how great the show was.

You don't know how many people I see when I'm signing autographs that say, hey, this place is great, I really enoyed the show, I haven't seen you in a long time, since you played the Spencer, Iowa, Fair, or some such place. In other words, the last time they saw me in person was when I had gone to their town to play. Now they've come to my town, to my theater, to see me.

I had a little old lady in here one night who was just so cute! She was thrilled to see me in person, bought a CD of mine and a cassette and had me autograph both of them. She told me, "I don't have a player for either one of these, but I've got to have them. I'll take them to my friend's house and listen." You talk about a compliment!

Today, Branson grosses more than two billion dollars annually. Sure, there are utilities and sewage problems, but that's all part of the growing pains. Right now there's eighty million dollars' worth of construction going on in Branson. I've heard there's interest in building a small Disneyland for all the kids that come here with their parents.

By making Branson my professional home base, I finally found the ultimate investment—myself. Doing so, I've been able to go from making a living to making a life. I hope that my success in Branson will allow me to pursue some of the other things I've always wanted to do. Although I made a low-budget comedy film with Mel Tillis in 1985, called *Uphill All the Way,* I'd still like to star in a dramatic motion picture and make a new type of recording. Rather than just going in and cutting a song, or several songs for an album, I'd like to do something with a theme, and really work on it until it comes out exactly as I envision it—a creative album that really says something.

I'd also love to do a play on Broadway. I did my first legit-imate musical in 1992, *Paint Your Wagon,* in Houston and Seattle. That's another thing I've always wanted to do.

Finally let me tell you that for all the possibilities I saw when I first came to Branson, Barbara had to be brought kicking and screaming to it. For one thing, she didn't want anything to take me away from Tulsa. For another, she was wary of my great intuitiveness when it comes to investments. Now, though, she feels completely different and is sure that Branson is part of "the plan."

What plan, you ask? Perhaps the best way to explain it is like this. About a year ago, Barbara and Rodney's wife, Karen, who is also a devout Christian, were sitting outside by the swim-ming pool. Suddenly, Barbara turned to Karen, and said, "It feels to me that there's a giant magnet over Branson, drawing up the hill the ones that are meant to be." And you know something? She was right. You may say, hey Roy, explain that last one a little more to me, and you know, I can't, other than to say I don't think anyone can really explain the phenomenon that is Branson. You just have to come and experience it for yourself.

And when you do, be sure to come by and say hello!

Fathers, Friends, Feelings, Family

10

It really bothered me when I was advised years ago that I had reached a point in my career where I was making more money in a single night than my dad did in a whole year. My first reaction was shame. I knew how hard he had always worked, and how it had forced him to regulate and guide his life a certain way, while all I had to do was hop on an airplane, fly somewhere, get my guitar out, and take home all this money. It took me a long time to understand I had nothing to feel ashamed about.

Along those same lines, I've often heard people say with some degree of resentment that entertainers are grossly overpaid. The more I understood how to deal with and accept my own success, the more I've learned why I really have to disagree with that way of thinking about a million percent. Although I've enjoyed fabulous success, I realize now that while our sacrifices are by no means comparable, I had to make as many of my own as my father did. If you look at what a performer does on stage, that's really his fun time. What goes into that hour and fifteen minutes of singing and playing is a lifetime of mostly unpaid preparation, study, practice, surrender, and sacrifice.

For instance, I've seen my own kids born, start school, and graduate from college. The difference is, because of my commitment to my career, I didn't get to see much in between. That always bothered me most in the summer and spring of those years when we had to play clubs seven nights a week and matinees on Sunday just to make enough money to keep food on the table, while other families gathered out by the patio, or in the backyard having big barbecues. I can remember so many times running off with my guitar while my neighbors sat there, waving, smiling, and asking me how I was doing.

I guess maybe that's one of the reasons I'm so proud of Barbara's son, Michael, who's now a surgical oncologist in Baltimore. I've never known where Mike picked up the desire to go into medicine. Ever since he was a tot he wanted to be a doctor, and he stuck with it. But hey, I thought the music business was rough! Getting into medical school, *that's* tough. First of all, you have to have the grades or you just don't get in. Second, there's the problem of quotas. With so many students from all over the world competing for a limited number of slots, a lot of times it's more a question of having to wait your turn than anything else. While Michael was waiting to enter medical school, he went ahead and got his master's degree from the University of Maryland.

I guess watching Michael grow up and become a success helped me understand my own father better, and although we were always close, somehow it made me want to get even closer to him. Let me try to explain. When I was growing up, I knew a lot of Jewish and Italian people, and one thing I always noticed was just how warm and affectionate these people were to other members of their family. Men hugged men, men kissed men, and there was nothing vile or weird about it.

I'd go out on the road, come home, I'd run in, hug and kiss my mother, but shake my daddy's hand. After a while it began to bother me that I couldn't do more. I wasn't Jewish or Italian, I was a fluorescent white-skinned Caucasian, a real-life version of George Carlin's hippy-dippy weatherman, and because of that, I thought, I wasn't allowed to be more affectionate toward my dad. For years, even when I would fly in and they'd be waiting for me at the airport, it was always the same thing, a kiss for Mom, a handshake for Dad.

Well, one day in 1982, I made up my mind a handshake wasn't going to be enough anymore. I was coming home from a long trip and hadn't seen my parents in quite a while. I taxied up in the airplane and saw them standing there. I shut the engine down, got out, hugged and kissed my mother, then walked up to my dad. As usual, he had his hand out. This time, I pushed it aside, hugged him and kissed him on the cheek. I felt him stiffen up just a little, and then relax. When I let go, I smiled and said, "Hey, how you doin', how's fishing . . . ," as if nothing had happened.

Not too long after, I went out on the road again, and when I returned, I got out of my airplane, hugged and kissed my mother, and went up to my dad, who had his hand out again. Once again I pushed it aside and hugged him and kissed him. He still didn't hug me back, but he didn't stiffen up either.

The next time I went to visit them, I got out of the airplane, Mom and Dad were standing there, and to this day I don't know where my head was. I walked up and hugged and kissed my mother, then went up to Dad and put my hand out. Without thinking, he pushed it aside and hugged and kissed me! Now, of course, we hug and kiss all the time, and I believe in my heart we're both better off for it.

I guess the lesson lies in understanding the nature of the different types of love we all experience. Learning not to be embarrassed to kiss my father was a big step for me and allowed something that happened to me years later while I was on stage to take place.

It happened in 1986. My family decided to surprise me by driving to Branson, without telling me, to see me perform in my own theater.

Oh, and did it ever blow my mind! There I was on stage doing my *schtick,* when I happened to look over and see this elderly man standing at the souvenir counter as if he's making a purchase. Something went off in my head, and I said to myself, gee, that fellow looks an awful lot like Dad. At that moment, he turned around and smiled up at me and I said, right into the mike, "Hey, that's my daddy!" I was completely speechless for fifteen minutes.

The people in the audience just got the biggest kick out of it when he came up on stage. I became very emotional when we hugged and kissed, and, when I finally found my voice I asked him what he was doing there. We played a song together, which was one of the biggest thrills of my life. Then he said my mother was out in the audience as well, along with Barbara, my brother, and my sister. Barbara, of course, had been in on the whole thing. That night I was reminded once again of the special power of family love.

Experiencing the love of true friendship is something else that has enriched my life. Going along with that, one of the problems of living a long time is that you start losing more and more of those people you've grown to love.

Roger Miller was one of my closest friends in the world. He and I knew each other almost from the very beginnings of our careers. We came along at about the same time and first met in 1964 in Nashville at something they used to call a "disk jockey convention" before it became the Country Music Association Awards ceremony.

Rex Allen, "The Arizona Cowboy," first put us together. There were constant parties going on at the convention that whole week, and Rex was having one in his suite. He invited a whole bunch of people up, including Roger and me. As soon as Roger walked into the room, Rex pulled me over to him and introduced us. No sooner did we shake hands than we just started right in on each other, bam, bam, bam, one-liner after one-liner. Rex knew both of us, knew we were both crazy, funny ad-libbers, and had purposely put the two of us together.

Once Roger and I discovered each other, we didn't separate for the rest of the week. We stayed together constantly, always trying to outdo the other, which made for some pretty fun times. He'd do a line, I'd do a line, the next thing we knew there'd be all these people around, watching us go at it, laughing, and applauding.

That's the way it stayed throughout the years. Roger lived in Los Angeles, and whenever I would be out there, friends would do anything and everything to get us together. We'd have big parties where everyone would sit back and just watch us cook. There was an underlying affection that formed the basis of our ongoing "Who can top the other guy" battle of wits.

Now, I like to think of myself as quick-witted, and I know Roger was, too. Often, when we were together, we would get into a groove and just go back and forth, rapid-fire. Our friends just loved to watch it happen, almost as much as we loved doing it.

One night, a couple of years ago, Roger came to visit me in my dressing room while I was appearing in Las Vegas, and we sat around for a while and chatted. Suddenly, I looked over at him and said, "Roger, I'm going to tell you something. Whenever we're around each other we get really silly. But I just want you to know that I love you." He looked at me sort of funny and said, "Well, I love you, too. *But we have to keep our sillies.*"

For a long time, I think, Roger was embarrassed to show his serious side, which was why he always believed he needed to "keep his sillies." Whenever things got too heavy, or he was hurting, he believed "the sillies" could get him out of it. I remember telling him one time, "You know, Roger, one of your songs I really love is 'When Two Worlds Collide.'" It's a very serious love song about a man and a woman meeting and their two worlds colliding. He said, without skipping a beat, "Oh, that's one of the worst things I ever wrote." He insisted "Dang Me" was a much better song.

Like Roger, I, too, had a problem with showing that "other" side of myself. For years, whenever I played "Malaguena," I'd cut up and clown during it, because I feared somebody would come up to me afterwards and say, "You're not serious about this, are you? You don't seriously think you're playing 'Malaguena,' do you?" And I would say, "Me? No, I'm just having fun!" Then, one night, about ten years ago, after a performance a guy came up and told me he really enjoyed the way I'd played "Malaguena." "But you don't need to clown it," he added, "it stands by itself." That really sunk down deep inside. From that day on I played it straight.

Toward the end of his life, I'm happy to say, Roger, who I

believe was a pure genius, finally learned not to be afraid of showing that "other" side, when he wrote the Broadway musical smash, *Big River,* based on *The Adventures of Tom Sawyer.* The success of that show promised to open a whole new world for him.

Who knows what heights he might have hit if he hadn't gotten sick. Toward the end, he had this big scar across his neck from throat cancer surgery. The last time I saw him, he wasn't able to sing anymore, but if he cocked his head to one side he could activate an artificial vocal chord that allowed him to "talk." I remember saying to him that was all well and good but how many gangster songs did he know?

He laughed and told me he was getting ready to write another Broadway show, to prove the first one hadn't been a fluke. Just before he passed away, he and his wife, Mary Arnold, the former female lead singer in Kenny Rogers's First Edition, moved to Santa Fe, New Mexico, and adopted a little boy and girl. Right up to the end, he was hoping to beat his illness and continue on with his career. He fought hard and long, and finally, I guess he just didn't have the strength left to keep on keepin' on.

His loss is a tragedy for all of us. Godspeed, you ol' hoss.

All my life, it seems, music has opened doors and gotten me into situations I would never have otherwise experienced. I have met and been asked advice by governors. I have sung for two Presidents.

I was invited to appear on a television special called "Country Music from Ford's Theater," to be taped on location in the Washington, D.C., theater where President Lincoln was assassinated. The guest of honor that night was President Carter. I had a kind of connection to the Carter White House. Billy, the President's brother, was a semiregular on "Hee Haw." I gave President Carter a lot of credit for not trying to sweep Billy under a rug. He was who he was, and in his way, the President was quite proud of his brother.

When I was a boy living in the Washington area, I used to go on school trips to Ford's Theater, and now here I was going back as an adult to perform there, before the President! The occasion was a special one for a lot of reasons, not the least among them was the fact that this was the first time a President had been in Ford's Theater since Lincoln's assassination. The entire theater had been refurbished, and the television show was being produced as a way to raise money for the Ford's Theater Foundation.

Because the President was there, the security was, as you might expect, extraordinary. We were all instructed to stay in specially designated areas, and not roam around backstage. When the show was over, nobody could do anything until the President was safely out of the theater and on his way. When it was time for me to go on, there was security everywhere as I went out on stage. I came out, bowed, then sat down on a stool with my gut string guitar and started singing:

> *Seems the love I've known*
> *Has always been the most destructive kind*
> *Maybe that's why now I feel so old*
> *Before my time . . .*
> *Yesterday, when I was young . . .*

Just at that moment one of the stage lights exploded, sounding for all the world like a gunshot! I closed my eyes and said to myself, *Why me, Lord?* as the Secret Service jumped up and reached under their arms for their Uzis and pistols. When I realized it was just a light, I kept on singing. There was a lot of movement, but not enough to stop taping. It was, without a doubt, one of the scariest moments of my life.

Thirteen years later, I was invited to do the same type of show at Ford's Theater for President Bush. I played two songs that evening, "Hey Good Lookin'" with the orchestra, and "Malaguena" on the twelve string acoustic. Ford's Theater is very small, and it felt as if the President were sitting right in front of me. As I'm playing "Malaguena" I could see he was just mesmerized. When I finished he gave me two thumbs up. You know, folks, it doesn't get much better than that.

As had been the case with the earlier Ford's Theater show, the performers were invited to the White House for lunch. Jimmy Dean had told me before the show that Bush was a very big fan of mine. Well, while I was on the receiving line, a marine officer asked me my name to tell the President. When he announced Mr. Roy Clark, the President looked up, and there was a flash in his eyes. "Hey, Roy," he said, "you're truly one of the great ones." We shook hands and visited a bit, he introduced me to Barbara, and then I went on. What a thrill for a simple country boy from Virginia!

Without question, there's a special kind of pride one feels being invited to play for the President. It goes to the very essence of what it means to be an American.

However, some of my greatest personal and professional moments have come in situations far removed from the glamour and the glory of the world stage. Let me tell you about one.

In 1974, I started a charity golf tournament in Tulsa. This was another idea for which I have to give Jim Halsey all the credit. He thought I ought to get more involved in the community. He's not a golfer, but he knew that I was, or at least try to be. We found a good, worthy charity, the Children's Medical Center. I've always been very child oriented, so it seemed a natural thing for me to be involved with the medical center.

Every year at the tournament many prominent guests come to contribute their name and time to this worthy cause, including Bob Hope, Jerry Lewis, Oral Roberts, Leslie Nielsen, Peter Marshall, and Dale Robertson, just to name a few. Even President Ford played in the tournament. As a result, we formed a friendship that has lasted through the years. During his 1976 bid for the presidency, one of the great thrills of my life was when I was asked to be an official greeter for the state of Oklahoma.

Always a very popular event at my tournament is the "pairings" party, where the entrants are put together with their celebrity partner. Usually the way tournaments are run, besides the gallery tickets that are sold to people who want to see the tournament in person, entry spots are bought by businessmen and corporations. For a donation of, say, five hundred dollars, they then get to play with a celebrity. We usually play a five-man scramble, five people on a team, four businessmen and a celebrity. It's an excellent way to raise money.

What's really fun is that it doesn't matter if the celebrity can actually play. Everybody knows it's a fun thing. It's not competitive, except for those guys who are Sunday afternoon golfers, who come there and are going to win even if they have to cheat! I'm always going around reminding them it's just a game, boys, just a game! Nevertheless, if they get beat out by a stroke, they have a tantrum! They throw clubs, they stomp, they cry. It's truly amazing!

Every year, before the tournament begins, I like to pay a visit to the Children's Medical Center in Tulsa, which brings me to my story. In 1983 I saw one little girl there, Davi Sallee was her name. She had been run over by a car, and almost every bone in her body was broken. She was comatose for a long period of time and the doctors told me they didn't think she would fully recover.

She was in a wheelchair, and seemed to be almost a vegetable. She was very frail, naturally, from being in a body cast for such a long period of time, and didn't have any control of her limbs. However, it was her eyes that really caught my attention. They were piercing, and unnaturally large, giving her face a look that reminded me of that famous photo of Anne Frank.

I immediately went over and started talking to her, and as I did her foot slipped off one of the wheelchair's pedals. I reached down and put it back, and as I did, said, "Oh, maybe I shouldn't have done that. It's not proper for boys to pick up girls' legs like that." Even though I knew she had no control over her mouth or facial expressions, I felt something coming from her, so I continued talking. "Besides, you could have done it yourself if you wanted to." With no change in her expression, she took her foot and moved it up and down.

Well, the nurses just went bananas! They said it was the first time she had made any movement since being admitted. From that day on, we kept in touch. Her condition began to improve, and she started writing letters to me. The nurses kept in contact with my office to keep me informed of her progress.

The next year, I returned to the medical center to present a check for the money we'd raised from our golf tournament. During the ceremony a nurse came up to me and told me when I was through there was a surprise waiting for me. I presented the check, talked to the press, and then as I was about to leave, looked up, and here was Davi Sallee walking down the aisle. She came right up and hugged me!

Davi's much better today, back in school and doing great. She's also very involved with the church, I guess because she knows it was the Lord who really healed her. He just used me as a little conduit, and allowed me the great privilege of being one of his messengers.

There have been moments when I've stopped and asked myself as I travel around and do my thing, is there any real reason why I get to do what I do? I know there are much better singers who are working as bakers and truck drivers. There are better guitar players who just play around the house or in small clubs. And there are much funnier comedians. So why me? Why was I singled out? A lot of the immensely talented people I started playing with back in Washington are still there. Why was I pulled out of that nest and given this road to success? There has to be a meaning to it all. And that's the reason I do things like golf tournaments for the Children's Medical Center. You see, when I witness miracles like Davi walking down that aisle, I suddenly understand the meaning of my life a whole lot better, and once again stop and thank the Lord for allowing me the privilege of being able to help others with the talent He gave me, using it in any way He sees fit.

Life in the Grand Ole Opry

11

When I won that banjo contest back in 1950, it was, as I mentioned earlier, the first time I had ever played at, or even *seen* the Opry. Years later, when I was on the D.C. nightclub circuit, a lot of Opry stars used to come up to play gigs, and Lord, it still seemed to me they were coming from somewhere remote, exotic, and distant, as far away and mysterious as the moon.

After that first appearance, for a number of reasons, I didn't play the Opry again for a lot of years, and because of the Opry's stringent performance code, I didn't become a formal member until 1988. The Opry's code used to insist a member couldn't miss two consecutive Saturday night performances. That rule had always been a point of friction between the artists and the Opry, because Saturday night is traditionally when the best major bookings are secured. A well-known performer can go out and make upwards of two thousand dollars on a good Saturday night, as opposed to working for the Opry at scale, which is still something like twenty dollars. As a result, for a long time many Opry performers simply ignored the rule, until about fifteen years ago, when a lot of members, including Kitty Wells and Chet Atkins, were let go.

Playing at the Opry has always been the ultimate prestige feather in every country performer's finest cap. There's simply no other place like it in the world. I guess the closest thing to it is the Louisiana Hayride, still a very large notch below. The Wheeling Jamboree, broadcast on "WWVA, from the rock-bound coast of Maine to the sunny shores of Florida," was, for a long time, also a major competitor, but nothing could ever really come close.

The Grand Ole Opry was, and essentially still is a radio program. A few years ago they started telecasting a thirty-minute segment on Saturday nights over TNN, and I have to say I think it's taken away a little of the Opry's mystique. I'll never forget the first night I heard Earl Scruggs with Bill Monroe at the Opry, when I was a boy back in Meherrin with my ear glued to the radio. In my mind I pictured a guy with fifteen fingers on one hand and three arms, because what Earl was doing on the banjo sounded physically impossible!

The Opry actually began as a radio show out of a studio at WSM. Listeners wanted to see it in person, so they just started dropping by the studio during the broadcast. Well, they started coming by in such numbers that the show had to move to a bigger studio. Eventually they needed a much larger facility, and moved first to the Belle Meade Theater, then the War Memorial Auditorium, followed by the Dixie Tabernacle, and finally to the Ryman Auditorium, before Opryland was built in 1974.

Although it's mostly a tourist attraction now, occasionally used for the taping of television shows, the Ryman will always be fondly remembered as the true home of the Opry. It was very uncomfortable, no air-conditioning, cold in the winter, unbearably hot in the summer, but nevertheless it was the spiritual home of Hank Williams, Uncle Dave Macon, Lefty Frizzell, Red Foley, Minnie Pearl, Rod Brassfield, Patsy Cline, Ernest Tubb, Loretta Lynn, Jimmy Dickens, Carl Smith, and Roy Acuff.

I started making regular guest appearances at the Opry during the early years of "Hee Haw," only after a friend of mine, Shot Jackson, who worked with Roy Acuff on and off for years, happened to ask why I never appeared on it. I told him I would love to, but that, except for the banjo contest, I'd never been asked. He said all he had to do was call Roy Acuff and ask him to put me on his portion of the show. We were sitting, just talking, and I said, you know, Shot, what I'd love even more would be to have my family, my dad and my uncles, play it with me. I thought that would be the perfect public thank you for all they had done for me in my life and career. "No sweat," Shot said. He called Roy Acuff, who said whenever my family and I wanted to do the Opry, it was fine with him.

I then called my dad, and asked him how he and his brothers would like to come on with me. I knew it was something he'd always dreamed about, but never really thought would ever happen.

Well, I'm happy to say that Roy Acuff did indeed have my family and me on the Opry. It was such a good appearance that after the show, Sam Lovullo came up to me and suggested we do it again, on "Hee Haw." That also turned out well, so much so that Jim Fogelson of ABC–Dot signed us to make an album of traditional instrumental country music. We called it *Roy Clark's Family Album,* and what do you know, it turned out to be my very first number one album!

Playing with my family at the Grand Ole Opry was what started me thinking that maybe it was time I became an official member of the mother church of country music.

I started dropping little hints around Nashville, and in 1988, Hal Durham, the general manager of the Opry, came to see me in my dressing room during a "Hee Haw" taping session. He said, "I understand that you would like to be a member of our family."

I told him that was true, and he said they would not only be very honored to have me, but that they realized at this point in my career I could probably do more for the Opry than the Opry could do for me.

I said, "Well, I don't look at it that way. We can do a lot for each other." To show their appreciation, they relaxed the Saturday night commitment for me, as they now have for others, making it possible for performers like Ricky Van Shelton, Garth Brooks, and Clint Black to all become members. We agreed that to satisfy my membership I would perform a minimum of twice a year, when I was in Nashville to tape "Hee Haw." As it turns out, I average about four appearances a year. Whenever I'm in Nashville, I always play the Opry.

With the passing of Roy Acuff, Minnie Pearl suggested I might be the logical choice to succeed him, and everybody associated with the Opry seemed to agree. I guess the powers that be figure I might be one of the few fellows around with a love for pure country music who could keep the image of Roy Acuff's Grand Ole Opry alive. I take as a great honor the fact that they think I might have those kind of credentials. No matter who eventually replaces Roy Acuff, the important thing is to keep alive the tradition of classic American country music and its greatest showcase, the Grand Ole Opry.

213

Even with the current revival of interest, there remain so many elements and so many parts of country music the mass audience is still unaware of, and that, in my opinion, is a real crime. Sure most folks know Hank Williams, but there are so many other wonderfully talented performers who never got the exposure or the recognition they deserved. When Ricky Skaggs and Ricky Van Shelton and Randy Travis hit it big, I was asked by a lot of publications what I thought of the new sound in country music.

New? Not to me. I think it's identical to what was popular when I first started. I honestly don't hear any difference, other than better recording techniques. To me it's the same nasal sound, same basic material, same subjects, same instrumentation. Don Helms, the original steel guitar player with Hank Williams, had a great line. He tells a story about how he was hired to do a Nashville session with a "country" group down from New York City, for use in a documentary film. He said he set his steel guitar up in the studio, and one of the guys from New York walked up to him and stared at his instrument. "Yes, it's a steel guitar," Don said. "They used to use 'em in country music!"

In my opinion, traditional country is an essential part of our great American heritage, something we have a right to be proud of, and should strive to preserve for our children to experience and enjoy, and children for generations to come.

In 1973, I was honored to receive the Entertainer of the Year Award from the Country Music Association, as well as the Academy of Country Music Association Entertainer of the Year Award. I may be the only performer who's ever won both in a single year. I normally don't put that much emphasis on awards, but I consider winning those two a milestone in my career.

I remember thinking the week before they were announced I had to be snake-bit because I was sure I wasn't going to win, and everyone was already congratulating me. Don't worry, people kept saying, you're a shoo-in. I finally figured the only reason I might actually have a shot was because everyone else who was worthy of winning had already done so!

Back then, the CMA put more emphasis on live entertaining. Nowadays, without question, the award is given to whoever has the biggest record of the year. If a performer wins Record of the Year and Male or Female Vocalist of the Year, he or she has a very good shot at winning Entertainer of the Year.

As with most major awards, there's a lot of wheeling and dealing that goes on prior to the actual announcements. If a performer has a major record label behind him, say, for argument's sake, Capitol, and another young star on Columbia would like to win the Horizon Award for the most promising new artists, his people might go to Capitol and say, look, you get all your people to vote for my guy as the Best Up-and-Coming Young Artist and I'll have all my people vote for your guy as Vocalist of the Year. Unfortunately a lot of that goes on and I think it takes away from the integrity of the vote. As a result, you can never be sure how much politicking went into your win. Still, there's no denying awards help your career.

Sonny James, a good friend of mine and a terrific performer in his own right, did what I thought was a great thing when I won. He took a full-page ad out in *Billboard* congratulating me for winning. It said:

For the first time the award has been won by a
true entertainer.

> Your friend, Sonny James.

After that, I started winning so many awards I thought someone had talked to my doctor and found out I wasn't going to
be around much longer! I was given my own star on the
Hollywood Walk of Fame, directly across from the famed Chinese Theater. I was immortalized at the Hollywood Wax Mu-
seum. We had the big unveiling of my likeness in a ballroom
at the Roosevelt Hotel. A friend of mine arrived late and
watched as they took the statue out and put it in the back of a
station wagon. His first reaction was, "My God, what happened
to Roy?"

I'm in *Guitar Player Magazine*'s Hall of Fame. I was voted
by their readership best country artist five years in a row, from
1976 through 1981. After five wins they automatically "retire"
you to the Hall of Fame. I won the *Playboy* Poll from 1977
through 1980 and then again in 1982. In 1980, Governor John
Dalton of Virginia proclaimed Roy Clark Day *and* Favorite Son
Day. I considered that a great honor.

Winning awards and being recognized is a great source of
pride for every performer, and I don't mean to trivialize either
their importance or my appreciation of them. However, among
the many I've won, let me tell you which "awards" I consider
among the most important to me.

The first is the Roy Clark Elementary School in Tulsa, Oklahoma. What happened was, a new school had been built and
several names for it were put up for nomination. Among them
were Mickey Mantle, because Mickey is from Oklahoma, and
me, Roy Clark. And, what do you know, the kids voted for me!

It was quite a thrill, because I've always been a strong sup-
porter of education. I believe in my heart the problems in
this world stem from widespread ignorance. People who
know more, are better educated, and have learned to make
choices can't be as easily led into self-destruction. A lack of
education is what makes the rise of a Hitler or a Saddam
Hussein possible. They specialize in putting hooks in people's noses and leading them around. If people were educated, they'd say, wait a minute, this is not good and I have
choices in my life.

So when the kids voted to name a school after me, I was
really blown away. I could picture in my mind little seven- and
eight-year-olds saying, "I go to the Roy Clark School!" I personally attended the dedication, and that day all the kids came
out of their classes to meet me. I also attended the school's
tenth anniversary and in my honor the children performed a
little "Hee Haw" skit. Each child was a different character,
dressed in bib overalls. One was me, one was Junior Samples,
and so on. It was such a kick!

Another "award" I cherish was one I received from a school
in Fayetteville, Tennessee, where I gave a concert to help raise
the money to build a field house. This high school had won
state championships in football and baseball, but didn't have
any sports complex on their campus for student practice or
play. Things had gotten so bad the students were forced to
dress in their classrooms, some even out in their cars. The
concert was a success, the field house was built, and they
named it the Roy Clark Field House. *I'd like to thank the
Academy* . . .

When Jim Halsey retired in 1990, I switched my management to John Hitt, whom I have known and worked with as

long as I've known Jim. John had worked for Halsey the entire thirty years I was there. Oftentimes Halsey would set up deals for me and John would coordinate them. In many ways, it's been John and me as much as Halsey and me for thirty years. When Halsey retired, he merged his agency with the William Morris Agency. I decided to go with John after he resigned from William Morris, and I've been very happy keeping our little "family" intact.

These days, when I'm not performing, I prefer to stay away from the central hubs of show business. That's probably why I've never wanted to live in Los Angeles or Nashville. I don't want to be in an environment where everybody talks about "the business." Everyone, in Hollywood, it seems, reads *Variety,* and in Nashville, *Billboard,* and every Monday morning breakfast begins with who landed what big deal. To tell the truth, I'd rather go fishing, drag race, or spend time with my classic car collection.

The Beatles wrote so many great songs, and I've recorded quite a few, but one line of theirs has always stayed with me. "And in the end, the love you make is equal to the love you take." That's always appealed to me, because love is the easiest thing in the world. I believe I was given the gift of love. I have been blessed in that I don't envy anyone. I don't want anything from anyone; I prefer to give. Maybe that's why I've had the longevity and success I've had.

To me, life is best when it comes down to the simple things. When I'm by myself, I'll still pick up the guitar and play just for the joy of it. At home, I keep one guitar by my chair, on a stand, and, even if I've been away performing for months, I won't be in that room two hours before I'll reach over, pick it up, and just noodle on it awhile. That's my friend. That's my buddy. It was with me in the beginning, and will be with me to the end.

Epilogue

*Intermission is over. The audience has re-
turned to their seats. The lights have gone
down, the spot is focused on center stage.
There is a spark of anticipation in the air. My fingers move
quickly, as if they have a life of their own.*

*The applause starts to build. I peek out around the curtain's
edge at the side of the stage. A full house. People have come to
see me. Some have been here before and have returned, like
old friends, to pay a visit. Others have never seen me in person,
and for them, this is the first night of my career. Some are
old-timers, retirees, golden anniversary celebrants. Others are
youngsters barely old enough to be in school. They all sit
together, waiting for me to begin my show.*

*As it has always been, their love and support is my cue to go
on.*

Index

Index

221

Index